The Gardener's
Hummingbird
Book

The Gardener's
Hummingbird
Book

By Val Cunningham

National Home Gardening Club
Minnetonka, Minnesota

ABOUT THE AUTHOR

Val Cunningham writes about nature, especially birds, from her home in St. Paul, Minnesota. An avid birder, she's out with her binoculars on a daily basis and enjoys traveling to birding hotspots in the United States and Central America. She is a nature writer and editor, and has been published in local, state and national newspapers and magazines. She takes particular pleasure in sharing with others her fascination with birds and birding. She and her husband maintain a backyard habitat for urban wildlife, particularly hummingbirds.

The Gardener's Hummingbird Book

Printed in 2004.

Tom Carpenter
Creative Director

Julie Cisler
Book Design & Production

Gina Germ
Book Production

Heather Koshiol
Managing Editor

On the cover: Ruby-throated hummingbird, male
On page 1: Black-chinned hummingbird, male
On pages 2–3: Rufous hummingbird, male

1 2 3 4 5 6 / 09 08 07 06 05 04
ISBN 1-58159-225-6
© 2005 National Home Gardening Club

National Home Gardening Club
12301 Whitewater Drive
Minnetonka, Minnesota 55343
www.gardeningclub.com

Photo Credits
Roger Aitkenhead/Animals Animals 39; **Francis & Janice Bergquist** 17, 18 (both), 25, 28, 32, 33, 36, 37, 42, 43, 45, 52–53, 56, 57, 91, 107, 158, 170, 171, 172, 174; **Greg Bergquist** 15, 19, 44, 64, 117, 124; **David Cavagnaro** 54, 66, 68–69, 73, 74, 75, 82, 99, 119, 121, 133, 135, 142, 143 (top), 145, 149; **Richard Day/Daybreak Imagery** 10, 16, 20, 23, 31, 34, 51 (right), 60, 61, 62, 84–85, 87 (top), 88, 115, 131, 132, 136, 140, 143 (bottom), 152, 159, 177 (left), 178, 179 (top), 138–139; **Susan Day/Daybreak Imagery** 103; **Saxon Holt** 55, 58, 59 (left), 70, 72, 76, 78, 79, 81, 83, 87 (bottom), 89, 95, 97, 105, 137, 147, 168, 179 (bottom), 169; **Maslowski Photo** 6, 30, 40, 41, 46, 63, 65 (both), 86, 122, 126–127, 128, 129, 130, 166–167, 173; **Jeff Milton/Daybreak Imagery** 59 (right), 161; **NHGC** 90; **NHGC/Tom Carpenter** 155, 156, 163; **Ralph Paonessa** cover onlay, 1, 2–3, 8–9, 12, 13, 22, 26–27, 29 (both), 35, 47, 49, 51 (left), 92–93, 177 (right); **Wendy Shattil/Bob Rozinski** 11, 96, 102, 109, 111, 112–113, 116, 123, 150–151, 160, 164, 175; **Stan Tekiela** 38.

Illustrations: Bill Reynolds/NHGC; maps: NHGC.

Special thanks to: Terry Casey, Janice Cauley, Michael Ferrier, Ryan Horner, Teri Lehner, Sandy Zilka.

Contents

Anna's Hummingbird, Male

Foreword

Welcome to the Beautiful and Magical World of Hummingbirds!

For such a tiny package, a hummingbird offers many thrills to observers fortunate enough to behold him at close range.

First, of course, there are those incredible wings; they beat so fast they buzz! Then consider the tiny bird's in-flight acrobatics—up, down, forward, backward, side-to-side, even hovering perfectly still in mid-air. And don't forget the colors, with males resplendent in their breeding finery and females adorned in subtle plumage no less impressive in terms of simple beauty.

But there's another aspect to the magic of hummingbirds, and it has to do with the places you find them: beautiful flower gardens, as well as natural places rich in nectar-producing blooms. You find hummingbirds in good places … the kinds of places that people like to be, too.

Couple those two factors together—magnificent birds that make your heart beat faster, colorful flowers that make you happy—and you have the makings of an intriguing pastime that can easily become a lifelong passion: gardening for hummingbirds.

It's fine to grow flowers for the sake of flowers. But when you can also attract something wild and beautiful to the garden you've created, the rewards are even sweeter.

Those are the ideas behind *The Gardener's Hummingbird Book*. Not only will you gain a better understanding of these intriguing and incredibly tough little birds, you will also see how to create a fine patch of habitat that is both pleasing to your eyes and attractive to the hummingbirds.

It's easy to attract hummingbirds to your yard and garden. With the right plans (found on the pages that follow) and a little energy and effort (you provide), you can create a haven for hummingbirds and people alike.

It's time to start the journey. Let this book be your guide … and then let the double joy of flowers and hummingbirds fill your heart.

INTRODUCTION

... where is the person who, on observing this glittering fragment of the rainbow, would not pause, admire, and instantly turn his mind with reverence ...

John James Audubon

Rufous Hummingbird, Male

We're All Hummingbird Fans

Humans are captivated by hummingbirds, and with good reason. They're drop-dead beautiful and endearingly miniature. Their dazzling colors lead some to call them the butterflies of the bird world. Their amazing flight ability has earned them the title of "feathered helicopters." Although hummingbirds are the smallest members of the bird family, they're not at all shy. Just the opposite, as a matter of fact: Many of us have had the experience of a tiny hummingbird whizzing within inches of our head, seeming to look us straight in the eye.

People—even those who aren't bird watchers—respond to hummingbirds. We enjoy their innate curiosity that leads them to explore every nook and cranny of our gardens in their search for new food sources. We admire their

Hummingbirds' dazzling color, tiny size and endearing acrobatics combine to captivate human fancy. Here, ruby-throated hummingbirds sip nectar from columbine flowers.

fearlessness and independence, even their pugnacious defense of a flowering shrub or nectar feeder. In many ways, they exhibit the possessiveness of the average toddler, with their "everything here is mine" attitude. They're here one second, gone the next, and their amazing speed and agility astonish us.

Hummingbirds have captured the imagination of humankind throughout time. They figure in the legends and ornamental robes of ancient Aztecs. The Spanish conquistadors called them *joyas voladoras*—flying jewels. On our own continent, hummingbirds gained legendary status as the "rain bird" among Southwestern Native Americans. And early English colonists of the New World, never having seen anything like them before, couldn't decide if hummingbirds were more like insects or birds.

Hummingbirds are so unlike other members of the avian world, with their bright, iridescent feathers, long bills and nearly invisible legs.

And they're so completely at home in the air, able to fly forward and backward and to hover near a nectar source or even, when startled, to fly upside down. Their diet is unusual among birds, with their devotion to flower nectar (although they have a carnivorous side, as well).

Hummingbirds are not known for their sociability and, indeed, seem almost to carry a chip on their small shoulders. Their fierce territoriality is the only thing large about them—

Hummingbirds have captured humankind's admiration for a long time. This Apache dancer's mask features a hummingbird to symbolize speed and agility.

Few fat reserves mean hummingbirds have to feed—a lot—to keep up with their frenzied metabolism. This male broad-tailed hummingbird drinks nectar at a thistle flower.

males spend a significant portion of each day driving away competitors. Males will battle other males, potential mates and even their own offspring to defend a prime feeding spot.

"Living large" seems to be a phrase invented perfectly for hummingbirds. Although most weigh much less than an ounce, they're among the toughest, most resilient members of the bird kingdom. They thrive in habitats as diverse as hot deserts and cold mountaintops. North American hummingbirds are found as far north as Alaska and the Yukon Territories and as far south as Florida. They accomplish astonishing

feats of athleticism, flying nonstop across the Gulf of Mexico or traveling thousands of miles each way between nesting and wintering grounds. And they've been observed harassing birds as large as hawks and bald eagles that dare to encroach on their territories.

Hummingbirds are fierce and feisty and live at a frenzied pace. It's been said that being a hummingbird is like driving a car with a one-gallon gas tank. They don't have much in the way of fat reserves, so they're not very well insulated. For this reason, hummingbirds must feed frequently during daylight hours and have developed a special adaptation to survive cold nights. They live their lives on the edge, trusting each new day to provide enough fuel to power their frantic lives.

Flowering gardens and hummingbirds are made for each other and most gardeners have a special affinity for these dashing, miniature creatures. At least one hummingbird species can be found in each ecoregion within the continental United States and southern Canada. Some areas are lucky enough to host several different species during at least part of the year. For most of us, the spring and fall migration periods are the times when we most notice hummingbirds, as they gratefully lap up nectar from our flowers and feeders and eat the insects they attract. Those of us who can provide each of the habitat elements that a hummingbird requires may even receive the ultimate reward: a hummingbird choosing to nest nearby.

This book will explore the world of the hummingbird, with life histories of the more common species and some fascinating aspects of their daily lives. We'll look at the plants that hummingbirds favor and some suggestions for creating a garden to catch their eyes and keep them coming back for more nectar. And we'll examine the value of nectar feeders and how they can complement even the most lavish garden.

What hummingbirds lack in size, they make up for in resplendent beauty. Depending on how the light hits them, they can instantly change from drabness to vibrant color, as in this handsome male rufous hummingbird of the Western mountains.

In the early 1700s, naturalist John Lawson published *A New Voyage to Carolina*, in which he wrote: "The Humming-Bird is the Miracle of all our wing'd Animals. He is feather'd as a Bird, and gets his Living as the Bees, by sucking the Honey from each Flower."

1

Hummingbirds: Fearless, Feisty and Gorgeous

Nature is painting for us, day after day, pictures of infinite beauty.

John Ruskin

Broad-Tailed Hummingbird, Male

Hummingbirds are unique in the world of birds. Everything about hummingbirds—other than their tiny size—seems larger than life. They're continually traveling in the fast lane as they go about their turbocharged days. At rest, a hummingbird's heart beats about 500 times per minute, or about eight times per second. When they're really fired up, such as when chasing a competitor or showing off for a female, a hummingbird's heart rate can jump to 1,200 beats per minute.

Hummingbirds' unusual wing construction and large flight muscles allow them to fly, at times, like insects, hovering here, zipping there and even turning somersaults in the air when startled. A hummingbird's wings beat so quickly that they're nearly invisible, appearing as a silvery sheen on each side of its body. Stop-

motion photography shows that ruby-throated hummingbirds *(Archilochus colubris)* beat their wings about 60 to 80 times per second as the birds zip from flower to flower. A broad-tailed hummingbird *(Selasphorus platycercus)* has been clocked beating its wings about 53 times per second while hovering. (Compare to a chickadee's 27 wing beats per second and a pigeon's eight beats per second.) Hummingbirds really rev up for their courtship and territorial dive displays, during which their wings may beat up to 200 times per second as they plunge in spectacular rage or ardor.

Although they feed throughout the daylight hours, hummingbirds quickly burn up much of the energy they consume, so they must feed frequently. Depending on the weather and the amount of nectar available, a hummingbird may visit from 1,000 to 3,000 flowers a day, launching itself on feeding forays every 15 minutes or so. They appear to be masters of the air with their acrobatic flight, but behind the scenes, their large flight muscles and

Without the modern miracle of stop-action photography, you'd barely see a hummingbird's wings. A blur is all you'd get, as with this rufous hummingbird at a feeding station.

whirring wings require a great deal of energy. Hovering in front of a flower to feed, something only hummingbirds can do, is even more costly in terms of burning up energy.

Lacking the stored fat and downy undercoat of other birds, hummingbirds have a unique way to survive during cold nights in spring or fall, especially at high altitudes. They turn down the thermostat to conserve their body's energy supply. This is called *torpor*, a state almost like hibernation. Heart rate and breathing slow dramatically, and body temperature drops to just a

Opposite: A hummingbird's wings beat 60 to 80 times per second in flight. It takes a fast camera shutter speed to freeze the action! This ruby-throat feeds at lantana.

few degrees above the air temperature. In torpor, hummingbirds expend very little energy, allowing them to survive cold nights. As the sun and the temperature rise, hummingbirds gradually rev up their internal engines. Once their body temperature rises to 86°F, a process that can take up to an hour, they're ready to fly off in search of breakfast.

A Metallic Shine

Hummingbirds' flashy plumage is another way they differ from other backyard birds. Some songbirds, including the common grackle (*Quiscalus quiscula*) and indigo bunting (*Passerina cyanea*) for example, have feathers that change color in the sunlight. But most hummingbirds have an even more spectacular look, with shiny, metallic-looking feathers over most of their bodies. The males' head and throat feathers are especially vibrant when they catch the sun and seem designed to attract a female's attention and intimidate rivals. The feathers covering hummingbirds' backs are also iridescent, but of another kind, so they tend to flash green in sunlight. As in other bird species, however, the females and young are usually much more drab than the males.

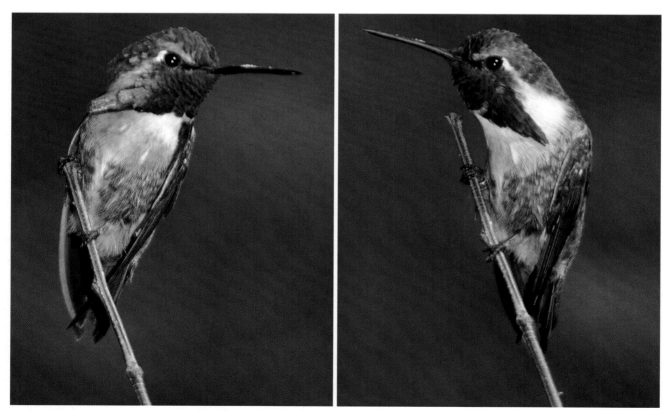

Light brings color to life. Compare the brilliant feathers on this male Costa's hummingbird (left) with the same bird perched in the shade (right).

A Rainbow of Color

A hummingbird in full sun exhibits a vibrant sheen, with its back, head and throat feathers flashing like molten metal. These are the hummingbird's iridescent feathers, and their color is caused by the way light interacts with the feather's structure. Within a hummingbird's bright, iridescent feathers are layers of air bubbles that bend and reflect the light. The color we see depends on two things: how much light strikes the feather and our viewing angle. A hummingbird in the shade may look dark and dull. But when the bird moves into sunlight, those drab colors (especially on its throat) undergo a dramatic change, now appearing as brilliant red, blue, green or purple hues. By contrast, a Northern cardinal's *(Cardinalis cardinalis)* brilliant red feathers are caused by a red pigment picked up from the food it eats. If you could grind up a cardinal feather, you'd have a small pile of red dust. A ground-up hummingbird feather, whose color is ephemeral, would produce a dusty gray residue.

Most of our backyard birds become airborne by using their legs to spring upward from a perch, but not hummingbirds—their legs are too short for this task. Instead, hummingbirds act like mini-helicopters, beating their wings rapidly for vertical lift-off. This is true even for female birds sitting on a nest. Brooding birds need to shift and change position frequently. Female hummingbirds accomplish this by beating their wings, rising several inches in the air as they turn, then settling back down on their eggs.

Now might be the time to consider why these birds are called *humming*birds. Think about your own experiences with hummingbirds and the answer springs to mind: We often *hear* them before we see them. Their rapidly beating wings give off a

Hummingbirds do rest. In fact, they spend more time perching than flying. This male broad-tail takes a break on a dead tree branch.

low-pitched humming sound that both precedes them and follows them as they zip out of sight.

Only in This Hemisphere

Hummingbirds are found only on our side of the world. Although other kinds of nectar-eating birds are found in both Africa and Australia, the Western Hemisphere is home to all of the world's 340 or so species of hummingbirds. Think of it: hundreds of different kinds of hummingbirds, in all sizes and colors, most living in the tropics, radiating out from the equator. The world's tiniest bird, Cuba's bee hummingbird *(Mellisuga helenae)*, is barely bigger than a bumblebee, measuring 2¼ inches from tail tip to end of beak. The largest, the aptly named giant hummingbird *(Patagona gigas)* found in Ecuador and Chile, is about the size of the gray catbird *(Dumetella carolinensis)*, measuring 8½ inches long.

Hummingbirds come in nearly every color and hue. In fact, renowned artist and naturalist John James Audubon described hummingbird feathers as "glittering fragments of the rainbow."

Opposite: To offer camouflage during their nesting duties, female hummingbirds have more earthy coloring than the flashy males, and exhibit a subtle beauty and grace all their own. These female ruby-throats feed on columbine.

Migration Seasons

Most hummingbird species seem to time their arrival in the spring just as the flowers they favor are coming into bloom. In the southern United States, this may mean hummingbirds arriving in January or February, while gardeners farther north start looking for hummingbirds in April and May. Hummingbird season starts even earlier for residents of the Southwest and Pacific Coast. And there are areas—the West Coast, the Southwest and isolated areas on the Gulf Coast—that host hummingbirds year-round. For example, the Anna's hummingbird lives throughout the year on California's Pacific Coast. Another hummingbird, the Costa's, can be found in every season of the year in southern California and southern Arizona.

Their names often suggest their wonderful and colorful diversity—there are sapphires and starthroats, topazes and emeralds, mountain-gems and sungems, firecrowns and woodstars.

Birds of the Tropics

The little dynamos are more at home in tropical regions, with the highest number of species found near the equator. Countries such as Ecuador and Peru each host up to 150 species of hummingbirds. However, species diversity (in both birds and plants) gradually decreases the farther north (and south) one travels, with Costa Rica hosting some 54 species, and Mexico just over 50.

The hummingbirds that migrate into the United States and Canada to breed, some 14 different species (with seven additional species making an appearance from time to time), spend six to seven months in the tropics each year. In late winter, their internal clocks compel the little birds to start heading northward. They go through frenzied eating periods to build up fat reserves, then embark on lengthy journeys of several hundred or even several thousand miles. The ruby-throated hummingbird, known for its spectacular nonstop flight across the Gulf of Mexico twice each year, increases its weight by about 50 percent before migration. The fat burns up quickly, so hummingbirds drop down frequently on land to refuel.

Songbirds accomplish similar feats of endurance, but hummingbirds are so much smaller (they're about one-third the weight of a warbler, for example) and they burn energy much more rapidly. Gram for gram, hummingbirds are some of the toughest, most resilient birds in the world.

Which Came First?

There's a kind of chicken-or-the-egg debate about hummingbird origins. Did they start out as insect-eaters or nectar-lappers? Although there's no fossil record to point

The green violet-ear hummingbird is just one of dozens of hummingbird species populating the tropical regions of our Western Hemisphere.

the way, some scientists suspect that the ancestor of the hummingbird was a tropical insectivore, an insect-eating bird. The theory goes that as these ancestor birds visited plants and flowers to glean insects, they picked up a taste for nectar. Over time, the birds evolved to consume both nectar and insects (and some plants evolved specifically to attract them; see Chapter 3).

Many people are surprised to learn that hummingbirds have a carnivorous side. But it's true: Hummingbirds eagerly consume gnats, aphids, other insects and spiders, often acting like miniature flycatchers when they encounter a swarm of gnats or fruit flies. They lap up the tiny insects they find inside nectar-bearing plants and search leaves, bark, pinecones and the surrounding air for others. Some hummingbirds "poach" spiderwebs, plucking out insects caught in the sticky silk. A healthy diet for a hummingbird is about three-fourths nectar and one-

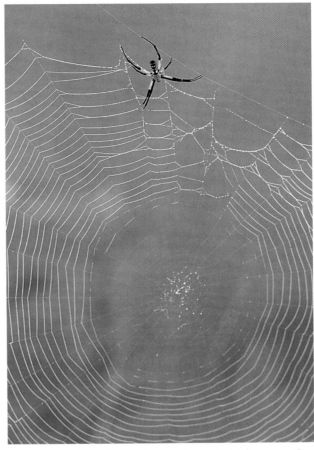

Insects are an important part of the hummingbird's menu. If this tiny spider gets away, a hummer will be happy to steal any gnats, aphids or other insects caught in its web.

fourth insects. The nectar provides energy and insects provide vital protein, vitamins and

Not Much for Singing

Hummingbirds are not rated among the noted songsters of the bird world. Instead, they produce a variety of almost insect-like squeaks, buzzes, chirps and hums. That distinctive humming sound is produced by their wings in flight. The birds can produce other sounds as well, by causing air to rush through their wings or tail. The broad-tailed hummingbird is known for the high-pitched trill made by its wings, while the Allen's (*Selasphorus sasin*) is noted for a metallic wing sound. Most songbirds—think of the American robin (*Turdus migratorius*) and the Baltimore oriole (*Icterus galbula*)—are known for the lovely songs they sing to establish a territory and attract a mate. Hummingbirds accomplish the same things through spectacular dive displays. The little birds rise high in the sky and then drop rapidly, tracing an oval, circle or J-shape in the air while emitting sharp sounds either through their feathers or vocalizations.

minerals for the little birds.

Among the hummingbirds that spend at least part of each year in the United States and Canada are the rufous *(Selasphorus rufus)*, Anna's *(Calypte anna)*, calliope *(Stellula calliope)* and Costa's *(Calypte costae)*. While our hummingbirds come in a wide range of colors and are so different from our songbirds, within the hummingbird world they exhibit striking similarities. The various North American species all have medium-length, straight beaks, brilliant head and throat feathers and all are fairly similar in size. Their nonmigratory cousins in Central and South America are much more variable. Some of these tropical birds have deeply curved bills, such as the white-tipped sicklebill *(Eutoxeres aquila)*, astonishingly long bills, like the green-fronted lancebill *(Doryfera ludoviciae)*, or surprisingly dull feathers, like the whole hermit family of hummingbirds. All of these are adaptations to local vegetation and conditions.

Tiny but Tough

Even though the majority of hummingbirds are nonmigratory, spending their lives in the tropics, they're not delicate little creatures. Instead, they're some of the hardiest birds on Earth, with some species living high in the Andes at up to 15,000 feet above sea level, where the nighttime temperatures often drop to freezing. In fact, many species of hummingbirds seem to favor mountainous regions, where the wide range of elevations offers greater diversity in flowering plants and habitats.

Hummingbirds exhibit astonishing strength, resilience and endurance. For example, the feisty rufous hummingbird leaves Mexico each spring and travels as far north as Alaska and the Yukon to take advantage of flowering plants and nesting sites. Some rufous hummingbirds cover up to 2,700 miles between their summer and winter homes. In a similar journey that takes place

Small but Courageous

Hummingbirds are fearless little birds, willing to take on just about any other living creature that approaches too near a food source or a nest. Hummingbirds chase away other hummingbirds, other kinds of birds, cats and dogs, humans and hawks, and there's even a report of a hummingbird buzzing a bald eagle that flew too low over its territory. The smallest birds in the world taking on some of the largest simply boggles the mind.

Hummingbirds apparently are emboldened by their maneuverability, speed and split-second ability to change direction. They exhibit no fear because they're sure they can fly out of any situation and avoid nearly all possible predators.

Opposite: Hummingbirds are tough and resilient—tiny packages built to withstand setbacks such as an early autumn snowfall. This immature calliope hummingbird was caught on his way down from the high country.

thousands of miles to the south, the green-backed firecrown hummingbird *(Sephanoides sephaniodes)* migrates from central South America and flies south to the tip of Chile each year to nest, then flies back to its winter home.

Each spring, migratory hummingbirds move up through Mexico by the millions. From the states along the U.S. border, they generally head north or northwesterly in a rush to claim the best feeding and breeding territories. Other millions of ruby-throated hummingbirds fly across the Gulf of Mexico and spread throughout the eastern half of the United States and southern Canada to raise their young. They all come in search of the burst of blooms and insects found in our temperate climate in summertime.

Our job as gardeners is to catch their eyes on this mad dash and tempt them down for a visit or even, if we're lucky, to entice a female to build a nest and raise a brood of nestlings nearby.

2

North America's Beautiful Hummingbirds

Understanding hummingbirds is the first step to enjoying and attracting them ... and appreciating their resilience and beauty.

**Black-Chinned Hummingbird, Male
At Trumpet Flower**

Most of North America's hummingbirds migrate, arriving in time to take advantage of summer's profusion of blooms and insects. This male broad-tail finds honeysuckle blossoms to his liking.

No matter how you look at it, North America isn't host to a great diversity of hummingbird species. We're a long way from the equator, where the highest number of hummingbird species are found. As the distance from the earth's middle increases, the number of species of hummingbirds steadily decreases—both to the north and south. Most of our hummingbirds are migrants, flying north through Mexico in the early spring. They follow traditional routes between Western mountain ranges or along coastlines that they've used for millennia. The one exception is the exceptional ruby-throated hummingbird *(Archilochus colubris)*, which crosses the vast Gulf of Mexico to reach landfall in the southern United States.

How many species can we count on our continent? It depends. One way to look at it is to focus on the birds that are known to nest here on a regular basis, since these are the birds that return every year. We know there's a "Big 8" species of hummingbirds that nest each year in the United States and parts of Canada (four of the Big 8 nest in southern Canada). These Big 8 are widely distributed across broad ranges. There are another eight species of hummingbirds that have been known to nest near the southwestern border of the United States or in Texas, some on a regular basis, some infrequently. Overall, it can be said that we have 16 species of hummingbirds that raise young in North America.

Then, if you add the other hummingbird species that are seen from time to time in the United States, the grand total can reach 21 hummingbird species. Whichever way we cut it, the total number represents only a small percentage of the 340 or so hummingbird species in the world.

Eight of these every-year nesters are widespread throughout the continent, occupying particular habitats within wide ranges. These are the birds that migrate from the tropics (or stay around all year) in order to breed and feed in our summer's abundance. These also are our most familiar hummingbirds and the ones we'll look at most closely in this chapter. We'll follow up with brief looks at some other species, then add descriptions of a few sporadic visitors. These species accounts are designed to pique your interest about the hummingbirds that may visit your region and your backyard.

The magnificent hummingbird—aptly named because of its color and size—is an occasional visitor.

Out of Their Jurisdiction

As recently as 20 years ago, ornithologists held pretty firm ideas about each hummingbird species' winter and summer range and migration routes. However, bird banders from coast to coast are adding some interesting new information to the mix, showing that some hummingbirds travel much farther and wider than has previously been thought.

Take the rufous hummingbird, for example: This bird of the West is a champion wanderer, frequently turning up in the eastern United States and even in eastern Canada during the winter. One recent year, there were reports of rufous hummingbirds from more than 25 states east of the Rockies. Other species that may make an appearance in fall and winter hundreds of miles to the east of their nesting grounds include the calliope, black-chinned, broad-tailed, Allen's and buff-bellied hummingbirds.

It used to be assumed that any bird so far out of its usual range was impaired in some way, but some species are appearing in winter with such regularity that researchers no longer make that claim. Bird banders and researchers are pondering this new aspect of hummingbird behavior. Theories include the effects of global climate change, the increase in the number of people who garden for hummingbirds and the availability of nectar feeders outside the blooming season.

One thing we do know: While the ruby-throated hummingbird owns the eastern half of the United States in summer, in winter it's just about any bird's game!

Ruby-Throated Hummingbird
(Archilochus colubris)

Male ruby-throated hummingbird.

Size: 3½ to 3¾ inches from tip of beak to end of tail; females are somewhat larger than males.

Habitat: prefers edge habitats found between woodlands and meadows.

Color: males have a red throat, black face, green head and back and a white front; females and young birds show green on head and back, grayish white on throat and breast.

Winter range: southern Mexico and Central America, with a few spending the winter in the southeastern United States, especially southern Florida.

Breeding range: regularly breeds across a vast swath east of the Great Plains; in Canada, its range reaches as far west as Saskatchewan.

Nesting season: late spring through summer.

Migration season: reaches southern United States in late February, northern edge of range in mid- to late-May; begins heading south as early as late July, continuing into late October.

YEAR-ROUND
BREEDING
WINTER

Ruby-throated hummingbird range.

A major portion of the United States and southern Canada plays host each year to a single species of hummingbird. The ruby-throated hummingbird "owns" the eastern half of the continent from the Atlantic Ocean to the eastern edge of the Great Plains and southward along the Gulf Coast during the summer. This striking bird, the only hummingbird known to nest east of the Mississippi River, has the largest range of any hummingbird species on our continent: It's found regularly in 38 states and seven Canadian provinces.

These superb athletes weigh only about one-tenth of an ounce, yet still manage to make their way each spring and fall across the vast Gulf of Mexico. Depending on their takeoff point, the tiny birds fly a distance of 500 to 600 miles, and it's all nonstop. (Those that don't use the water crossing take the long way around, over land.) The eastern half of the continent features a fairly similar topography and climate in summer, lacking the kind of variation that would support a greater variety of species. Although ruby-throats are the only hummingbirds to inhabit this range in summer, there are increasing reports of Western species wandering eastward in the fall and winter.

Female ruby-throated hummingbird.

Rufous Hummingbird
(Selasphorus rufus)

Male rufous hummingbird.

Size: 3¼ to 3¾ inches in length.

Habitat: woods along stream beds, forest edges, coniferous forests.

Color: males are mostly red-brown with bright green crown, iridescent scarlet throat, some white below (young males and adult females may have a few bright throat feathers); females and young have coppery flanks, whitish throat and breast, bright green head and back.

Winter range: southern California coast and Gulf Coast states to south and south-central Mexico.

Breeding range: northern Pacific Coast as far north as southeastern Alaska.

Nesting season: April to July.

Migration season: begins in February, reaches northern edge of range by late May; southbound migration begins as early as June and continues into October.

YEAR-ROUND ■
BREEDING
WINTER ■

Rufous hummingbird range.

The rufous hummingbird is the common backyard hummingbird of the Pacific Northwest. This "bad boy" bird, known for its feisty and aggressive behavior, has one of the longest migratory routes of all hummingbirds, with some traveling almost 3,000 miles in spring and fall. Winters are spent in Mexico and summers find the rufous as far north as southeastern Alaska and the southern Yukon, the farthest north of any hummingbird.

Rufous hummingbirds migrate along a corridor between the Pacific Ocean and the Great Plains. Early in the year, they hug the western edge of this corridor, primarily along the Pacific Coast. After nesting season, many head inland, through the Sierras and Rocky Mountains, taking advantage of mountain meadow blooms.

Like its cousin the ruby-throat, rufous hummingbirds often arrive on northern breeding grounds ahead of the blooming season and rely on insects and sap wells drilled by sapsuckers to tide them over until nectar is available.

Female rufous hummingbird.

The wings of adult males produce a distinctive metallic buzz, and they chatter incessantly to drive other birds from their territories. This species is named for the bright cinnamon plumage found on both males and females.

Although they usually follow a north/south migration route, rufous hummingbirds are known to wander. In the late fall, many vagrants found east of the Mississippi River are rufous hummingbirds. Increasing numbers are spending the winter along the Gulf Coast and in the southeastern United States, some returning year after year.

Black-Chinned Hummingbird
(Archilochus alexandri)

Female black-chinned hummingbird.

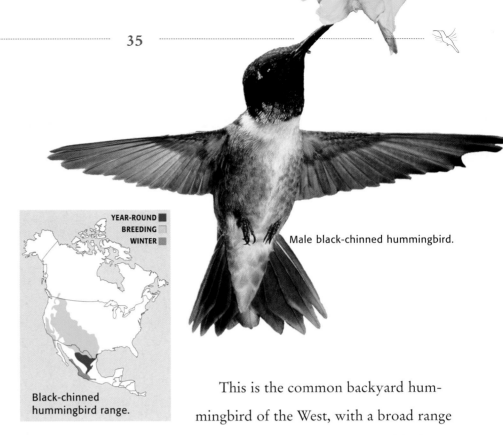

YEAR-ROUND
BREEDING
WINTER

Black-chinned
hummingbird range.

Male black-chinned hummingbird.

Size: 3¼ to 3¾ inches long.

Habitat: favors lowland woods along creeks and streams and desert scrub.

Color: males have black head and chin bordered by seldom-seen purple band, contrasting white chest, green sides and dull green back; females and young birds are green on back with pale gray underparts and dull green sides.

Winter range: Mexico, with a few birds spending winters in coastal south Texas and in the southeastern United States.

Breeding range: much of the West up to south central British Columbia, south to central Mexico and east through western two-thirds of Texas.

Nesting season: April through August.

Migration season: early March through mid-May in spring; fall migration begins in July, peaks in late August and continues through late October.

This is the common backyard hummingbird of the West, with a broad range extending from California to Texas during the summer. The black-chin's breeding range also includes eastern Washington and portions of Idaho, Montana, Wyoming, Colorado and New Mexico. Since black-chins prefer low elevations, these birds aren't found in the high mountains during nesting season. Female ruby-throated and black-chinned hummingbirds are very similar in appearance. Because the two are difficult to tell apart, it's lucky their breeding ranges have so little overlap.

The black-chinned is one of the least splashy North American hummingbirds, named for the dark head and chin of adult male birds. The male's brilliant purple chin band is gorgeous but seldom visible. Black-chins are known for their rapid tail flicks or wags as they hover to feed.

Black-chinned females are very hardy birds and often start building a second nest and incubating eggs while still feeding young birds from the season's first nest. The birds are feisty, like all hummingbirds, but black-chins are not the most dominant of species. If a competitor takes over its feeding territory, a black-chin often resorts to thievery, dashing to a food source such as hanging feeders or flowers for a quick drink, then quickly moving on.

Broad-Tailed Hummingbird
(Selasphorus platycercus)

Male broad-tailed hummingbird.

Size: 3¾ to 4¼ inches.

Habitat: woodlands, mountain forests and meadow edges.

Color: males have bright pink throats and brilliant green backs and crowns, with white below; females and young birds have bright green backs and crowns, some rufous shading on sides, with throat feathers showing some small spangles.

Winter range: Guatemala and Mexico, with a few found along the U.S. Gulf Coast.

Breeding range: nesting range covers 12 states, from California to west Texas and Idaho south to Arizona.

Nesting season: April to August.

Migration season: late February into May; southward migration begins as early as July and continues into October.

YEAR-ROUND
BREEDING
WINTER

Broad-tailed hummingbird range.

This is the mountain hummingbird of the West, often seen feeding in high-elevation meadows even above 10,000 feet. Broad-tails have one of the loudest wing sounds of all hummingbirds, with adult males producing a high-pitched whistle with their wings. This continuous trilling probably serves to warn competitors to stay out of a broad-tail's territory.

Adult male broad-tails closely resemble male ruby-throated hummingbirds, but geography and that distinctive wing trill can be used to identify the two birds. This is the largest of the eight species widespread in the United States, often measuring slightly more than 4 inches from head to tail.

Broad-tails are used to cold temperatures and move to successively higher elevations as flowers come into bloom. They often arrive early in spring, while there is still snow on the ground and nectar is not yet widely available. These "early birds" rely on tree sap in sap wells drilled by sapsuckers and on insects for food in early spring. Females often encounter fairly rugged conditions during nesting season, sometimes enduring nighttime temperatures below freezing, so they must feed heavily each evening to survive the night.

This species is not known for its aggression and is easily dominated by fiercer birds. This may explain why they generally are found at such high elevations in this country, where there are few competitors. Interestingly, not all broad-tails travel to the United States to breed. A population remains in the mountains of Mexico and Guatemala year-round.

Female broad-tailed hummingbird.

Allen's Hummingbird
(Selasphorus sasin)

Male Allen's hummingbird.

Size: 3¼ to 3¾ inches.

Habitat: wooded coastal lowlands and forests, often near streams and rivers.

Color: males have bright green back and crown, iridescent red-orange throat, cinnamon sides and rump, white below; females and young birds are green on the back and head, with cinnamon sides, white breast and whitish throat with reddish or bronze spangles.

Winter range: mainly southern Mexico, although a few remain in southern California or fly to Southeastern states.

Breeding range: along Pacific Coast from southern California to southern Oregon.

Nesting season: mid-February to early July.

Migration season: arrives on nesting grounds January through March; departs mid-May through September.

YEAR-ROUND
BREEDING
WINTER

Allen's hummingbird range.

Named for an early naturalist, the Allen's is one of two hummingbirds common to northern California gardens (the other is the Anna's). The Allen's has a restricted breeding range, favoring a narrow belt of land along the Pacific Coast from southern Oregon to southern California. A nonmigratory population remains year-round on the south California coast and on the Channel Islands.

Like the broad-tailed and rufous hummingbirds, the male Allen's produces a metallic buzzing wing sound. The Allen's migrates much earlier than other species of hummingbirds, arriving in California as early as January. This, plus the mild coastal climate, gives the birds a longer nesting season than most species, and many Allen's females raise two broods a year. A map of their migration route, spring and fall, traces an oval pattern, proceeding up the West Coast in early spring and returning through the Sierras in late summer.

With its cinnamon sides and red throat, the Allen's looks a great deal like the rufous hummingbird, but the green back of the adult male Allen's helps differentiate it from its close relative. Not quite as aggressive as the rufous, the Allen's is also a bit shy, preferring not to nest in yards and gardens. In May and June, when many songbirds are just beginning to arrive on their summer grounds, the Allen's is already starting its southward migration.

Female Allen's hummingbird.

Anna's Hummingbird
(*Calypte anna*)

Female Anna's hummingbird.

Size: 3½ to 4 inches.

Habitat: nests in dense evergreen thickets, small trees and streamside woods and parks and gardens.

Color: males have bright green back and rose-red throat and crown, underside is pale gray with green sides; females and young birds are bright green above, pale gray below, with some mottled reddish or bronze throat feathers.

Range: only semi-migratory, found year-round from Vancouver Island, British Columbia to Baja California, although they may retreat from northern-most areas in winter.

Nesting season: November to May in California, October to June in Arizona, February to June in the north.

Migration season: many Anna's leave nesting areas from May to November and can be found in mountains of Arizona and California from late summer to fall.

YEAR-ROUND ■
BREEDING
WINTER

Anna's hummingbird range.

The Anna's was named for Anna Masséna, Duchess of Rivoli, wife of a noted 19th century French collector of bird specimens and herself a supporter of the natural sciences. Two things make the Anna's stand out among North American hummingbirds: First, they're less migratory than other familiar species, found year-round from southeastern Arizona to California and as far north as Vancouver Island, British Columbia. Second, they're among the best-known singing hummingbirds, although the male's song has often been described as "unmelodic."

The Anna's is the backyard garden bird of the Pacific Coast, although they are now expanding their range northward and eastward as far as southwestern British Columbia and west Texas. Some of this range expansion may be due to the increase in gardens featuring exotic plants and nectar feeders that provide new sources of food. Since the Anna's doesn't need to travel to nesting grounds, its breeding season begins earlier than migratory hummingbirds'. In the southern part of their range, they may begin nest building as early as October, and many Anna's will be sitting on nests by New Year's. Their early start gives them time to raise two or three broods during nesting season.

After nesting, many Anna's wander into the mountains or farther eastward in the summer, but they're not traditional migrants. Interestingly, insects make up a larger portion of their diet than in some other species.

Male Anna's hummingbird.

Costa's Hummingbird
(Calypte costae)

Size: 3 to 3½ inches.

Habitat: dry washes, chaparral thickets, hilly terrain with cactus.

Color: males have purple crown and throat, green back, white breast and green sides; females and young birds are bright green above, pale gray below, often with a few iridescent feathers on the throat.

Year-round range: southern California to south-central Arizona.

Breeding range: same as year-round range; some birds move farther north and east.

Nesting season: possibly as early as December, but generally mid-February to mid-April.

Migration season: some movement in January and February; after nesting, some birds move inland and into the mountains before retreating; southward movement in September and October.

YEAR-ROUND ■
BREEDING ▨
WINTER ▨

Costa's hummingbird range.

This small and elegant bird is named for a French aristocrat with a large hummingbird collection. The Costa's is the desert hummingbird, choosing to breed in hot, dry climates like that found in the Mojave and Sonoran deserts. The Costa's makes its nest far from sources of water and is not often found in backyard gardens. The sparse vegetation in the dry washes and chaparral habitats where Costa's live forces them to defend large feeding territories, up to four acres in some cases. The Costa's is a year-round resident from southern California to southern Arizona.

The males' vibrant purple throat feathers have an unusual, elongated shape, extending out to the sides, even slipping back over their shoulders in flight. (These feathers remind some of the luxuriant mustache of the zany cartoon character Yosemite Sam.) The males' courtship dives and whistles are spectacular and Costa's are among the most territorial of hummingbirds—until they bump up against an Anna's. The two species are closely related and their ranges show some overlap. The Costa's is being edged out by increasing urbanization in some areas—a development which doesn't seem to deter the Anna's.

Male Costa's hummingbird.

Well adapted to hot, dry regions, Costa's often perch in the shade for long periods on the hottest days. They probe everything from tiny desert lavender *(Hyptis emoryi)* flowers to giant saguaro cactus blooms for nectar. A favorite nectar source for the Costa's is the chuparosa shrub *(Justicia californica)*. These small, bright birds are on the move once breeding season is over, although little is known about their summer travels. They may head for higher elevations to find new sources of nectar.

Calliope Hummingbird
(Stellula calliope)

Male calliope hummingbird.

Size: 2¾ to 3¼ inches.

Habitat: high-elevation coniferous forests and streamside willow and aspen thickets.

Color: males have brilliant magenta and white throat, bright green back and head, white below, green on flanks; females and young birds have bright green on head and back, white below with cinnamon on flanks, some spangling on throat feathers.

Winter range: southwestern Mexico, increasingly along Gulf Coast.

Breeding range: much of the northern West, including British Columbia, western Alberta and the mountains of southern California.

Nesting season: mid-May through July.

Migration season: begins arriving in southern California in March, reaches northern limits of its range in May; begins southward journey in late July, continuing through September.

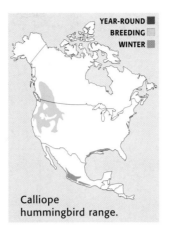

YEAR-ROUND ■
BREEDING
WINTER

Calliope
hummingbird range.

This smallest of our nesting hummingbirds (imagine a bird that weighs less than a penny) is also the smallest bird of any kind on the continent. Some calliopes measure less than 3 inches long, while most other familiar hummingbirds are 3½ to 4 inches long. This is a bird of the mountains, nesting at high elevations, then moving upward as summer progresses and new flower sources come into bloom. In some cases, calliope hummingbirds have been found nesting near the timberline above 10,000 feet.

The male's throat patch is unique, with magenta-red streaks against a white background. The throat feathers can be fanned out when males are excited, creating an amazing, streaky starburst pattern. The calliope frequently feeds close to the ground and often visits sapsucker wells early in spring. These tiny birds survive among larger hummingbirds and males can be fairly belligerent, holding their own even against the more savage rufous. They're known for cocking their tails while hovering.

Calliope females take nest fidelity to the extreme, often building a new structure on top of the old one, sometimes creating a tower of up to four nests. They often nest in pine trees, even building on top of pinecones. Females are very protective and will dive-bomb squirrels and even humans that approach a nest too closely. The calliope is not a common visitor to urban and suburban backyards, except during migration.

Female calliope hummingbird.

Other Hummingbird Species Found in the United States

Within limited geographic ranges, mostly in the Southwest.

Blue-Throated Hummingbird
(*Lampornis clemenciae*)

YEAR-ROUND ■
BREEDING □
WINTER ■

Blue-throated hummingbird range.

At 5 inches, the largest hummingbird in the United States; found near streams in mountain canyons along the Mexican border from western Texas to southeastern Arizona. Adult male has distinctive blue throat and is very aggressive.

The blue-throated hummingbird is the largest hummingbird to venture into the United States. This male sits atop a century plant.

Sending a Message

Hummingbirds engage in showy behaviors designed to impress a possible mate or intimidate intruders and competitors. Each species has its own specific courtship dive, with a specific pattern and height. Take the Anna's hummingbird, for example: A male quickly flits high in the air, then plummets toward the ground at up to 65 m.p.h., emitting a loud squeak as it passes near another bird.

Other hummingbird species are known for their U-shaped or J-shaped dives (the calliope, for example), an oval (the rufous) or the spiraling climb-and-dive of the Allen's. Most hummingbird dive displays are quite noisy, accompanied by whistles, buzzes or squeaks, produced either vocally or by air whistling through feathers.

Hummingbirds also send visual messages through something called a shuttle display. A perched male bird may sway back and forth, showing off his throat feathers. Or a male will fly back and forth horizontally, above or in front of another bird to impress or intimidate. Two ruby-throats may fly up and down like little elevators, each trying to drive the other away.

Birds will fan their tails at rivals and perch with sunlight striking their throat feathers at exactly the right angle for maximum color reflection.

They're small, but they're crafty.

Magnificently colored broad-billed hummingbirds (like the male pictured here) occasionally show up in southern Arizona.

The Superlative Problem

When we take a quick look at hummingbird physiology, we inevitably bump up against one problem: The way these little birds operate is almost beyond our comprehension. Can they *really* breathe up to 250 times a minute while resting on a branch? When they're chasing a rival or performing a spectacular courtship display, is it possible that their hearts race up to 1,200 beats a minute? The answer is yes, on both counts.

As for the whirring wings for which they're named, it wasn't until the advent of stop-motion photography that hummingbird wingbeats could be counted. Again, the numbers are astonishing, ranging from 60 to 80 flaps per second for the smaller hummingbirds in normal flight, then up to 200 times per second while performing dive displays.

Proportionately, hummingbirds have the largest flight muscles in the bird world, averaging a fourth to a third of their total body weight. These small birds need plenty of muscle to power their high-energy aerial maneuvers.

YEAR-ROUND ■
BREEDING ■
WINTER ■

Broad-billed hummingbird range.

Broad-Billed Hummingbird
(*Cynanthus latirostris*)

One of the most colorful hummingbirds, with bright green backs and males' deep blue throat; both genders have a bright red-orange bill with a black tip. Range is limited, but where found, they're abundant at low to middle elevations in south-central Arizona.

Buff-Bellied Hummingbird
(Amazilia yucatanensis)

YEAR-ROUND
BREEDING
WINTER

Buff-bellied hummingbird range.

This tropical hummingbird found in southeastern Texas and the Rio Grande Valley has a buff-colored stomach, bright green head and breast and distinctive bright red beak. Some move north and eastward to winter in coastal Louisiana, Mississippi, Alabama and western Florida.

That Persistent Goose Rumor

One of the most persistent myths surrounding hummingbirds is the one that says they migrate on the backs of geese. It's not hard to understand how such a rumor got started: Hummingbirds' tiny size leads us to think of them as delicate, so it's difficult to believe they're capable of the spectacular feats of athleticism required to fly up to thousands of miles twice a year. But they do it, and without any help from geese.

Geese migrate at different times than hummingbirds do, and their winter homes are hundreds or even thousands of miles from the tropics where most hummingbirds spend the winter. No, geese don't provide a limousine service for hummingbirds. Instead, the real story is even more amazing. Tiny as they are, hummingbirds power their own migration, using internal calendars and compasses, as well as fat stores and food found along the way.

Buff-bellied hummingbirds, like this handsome male, occasionally make their way into the valley of the Rio Grande as well as the southernmost sections of the Gulf Coast states.

Lucifer Hummingbird
(Calothorax lucifer)

This Southwestern visitor with its bright purple throat can be distinguished from other

YEAR-ROUND
BREEDING
WINTER

Lucifer hummingbird range.

hummingbirds by its long, curved bill; an uncommon-to-rare nester in southeastern Arizona, southwestern New Mexico and western Texas.

The lovely violet-crowned hummingbird occasionally makes appearances as far north as southern Arizona.

Magnificent Hummingbird
(Eugenes fulgens)

The male has a nearly black belly, bright

YEAR-ROUND
BREEDING
WINTER

Magnificent hummingbird range.

turquoise chin feathers and purple head, while the emerald-colored female is known for her dark face and ragged white stripe behind the eye. This second-largest U.S. hummingbird (up to 5 inches) can be found nesting in the Southwest's "sky island" mountains (tall, scattered peaks in the desert).

Violet-Crowned Hummingbird
(Amazilia violiceps)

YEAR-ROUND
BREEDING
WINTER

Violet-crowned hummingbird range.

The violet-crowned's violet-blue crown, bright orange beak and bright white throat and underparts make it a standout. Still quite scarce, it is mostly found in southeastern Arizona, where it may overwinter if feeders are available.

White-Eared Hummingbird
(Hylocharis leucotis)

This bird is named for the bold white line extending behind each eye; rare in summer in a few canyons in Arizona's "sky island" mountains and even more rarely found as far east as west Texas.

White-eared hummingbird range.

Berylline Hummingbird
(Amazilia beryllina)

This is probably the least common U.S. nester; found rarely in southeastern Arizona and Texas's Big Bend region. Named for the gemstone, males and females have similar bright green plumage.

Berylline hummingbird range.

Sporadic United States Hummingbird Visitors

- **Plain-Capped Starthroat** *(Heliomaster constantii)*: found occasionally in southern Arizona.

- **Green Violet-Ear** *(Colibri thalassinus)*: wanderer from tropical Mexico.

- **Green-Breasted Mango** *(Anthracothorax prevostii)*: rare visitor to Gulf Coast and southern Texas.

- **Bahama Woodstar** *(Calliphlox evelynae)*: extremely rare visitor to southern Florida.

- **Xantus's Hummingbird** *(Hylocharis xantusii)*: extremely rare, West Coast.

Raising Young Hummingbirds

Hummingbird females build a nest, then, almost invariably, lay two tiny, navy-bean sized eggs. Female birds handle all the duties of incubating eggs, feeding young birds, cleaning up after them and teaching them the ropes by themselves. Eggs are usually incubated for about 15 to 20 days, then the miniscule, naked young hatch. One ornithologist has called them "ugly, unpromising little grubs."

For the first three weeks or so, the mother bird feeds her twins a slurry of nectar and tiny insects. When they're very young, she may feed them up to 15 times every daylight hour. At about two and a half weeks, the young twins are fully feathered and their bills have begun to elongate. Even after the young have left the nest and begin to roam, sometime after the third week, the diligent mother bird continues to feed them for another two to four weeks.

Above: A hummingbird nest is about the size of a walnut shell, and is camouflaged expertly with woodland lichens. A pair of eggs—each the size of a navy bean—rests inside.
Left: A Costa's hummingbird mother feeds her chicks a slurry of nectar and tiny insects.

3

Attracting Hummingbirds: The Basics

The two most popular leisure-time activities in the United States are gardening and bird watching. Double your enjoyment of the outdoors by combining the two into a magic combination: gardening for hummingbirds.

Costa's Hummingbird, Male
At Lantana

Plant a flowering garden, and they will come. Even if you've never seen a hummingbird in your area before, hummingbirds almost surely have been around, especially during spring and fall migration periods. Every garden in the United States and southern Canada has at least one hummingbird species flying over it. If you put out the welcome mat, you can entice hummingbirds to drop in and stay a while. Gardens that fulfill a hummingbird's habitat needs may be rewarded by a female choosing to nest nearby or a feisty male defending the backyard as his summer feeding territory.

There's not much mystery about what will attract hungry hummingbirds: They're looking for the quick energy burst that nectar gives them. To find a sweet drink, they'll probe the flat-faced blooms of a clump of impatiens (*Impatiens* spp.) and the long, tunnel blossoms

Color is the key to attracting hummingbirds. Red is great, but any intense hue can do the job. In this case, it's a bountiful basket of magenta-colored impatiens.

Which Came First?

When hummingbirds first appeared on the planet, did they survive by drinking nectar or by eating insects? We think of them as spending their time foraging among nectar-producing plants, but this may not always have been the case. Some bird scientists regard hummingbirds as insectivores whose insect hunting is fueled by nectar. This theory says that hummingbird ancestors probed plant blossoms for tiny insects and came to develop a taste for the nectar the insects fed on.

As plants evolved to attract hummingbirds (and discourage all but the tiniest insects), the birds adapted to better reach inside flowers for nectar and insects. Over time, the birds' beaks lengthened, their bodies became more miniaturized for maneuverability and their wings and wing muscles evolved to meet the demands of hovering flight.

It's clear that these small birds couldn't survive on sugar water alone. Nectar provides a quick energy burst, but the birds must look elsewhere for protein, vitamins and minerals. Insects provide the energy to power muscles, produce feathers and help build a layer of fat for migration. Nectar makes up about three-fourths of hummingbirds' daily calorie intake, with the other one-fourth coming from insect consumption.

of the trumpet creeper (*Campsis radicans*) and just about everything in between. The tiny insects and spiders that hummingbirds need for protein, vitamins and minerals are often found near good nectar sources, as well. Yes, these tiny birds are also carnivores, avidly plucking insects from the air, plant leaves, tree bark and flower cavities. If your garden provides nectar to drink and insects to catch, there should be hummingbirds around, at least during migration.

Catch Their Eyes

Red is the first color to catch their eyes, so having red-blooming plants or shrubs serves the same purpose as a highway billboard advertising a good restaurant nearby. If hummingbirds are migrating through your area, red will make them slow down, look over your garden and drop down to visit. It's estimated that a hummingbird in flight can spot a red flower from half a mile away. Once they come down to

Tubular flowers—such as these blossoms on a trumpet vine—are thought to hold more nectar for hummingbirds. Combine "tunnel" blossoms with the color red and you have a great hummingbird plant.

hover in a garden or mountain valley, however, the little dynamos will visit a wide range of flower colors, not only red ones.

Interestingly, studies of hummingbird feeding preferences show that after the initial attraction, a flower's color is not the most important factor to the birds. First, they assess whether a plant and its flowers are easy to reach. Think of foxglove (*Digitalis* spp.) and honeysuckle (*Lonicera* spp.) plants and how they make it

easy for hummingbirds to move from bloom to bloom without tucking their wings. Next in line for consideration is the amount of sugar in the flower's nectar. They won't come back if the sugar concentration dips below about 12 percent, and they seem to prefer 20 to 25 percent sugar in their nectar. Flower color is ranked third and seems to operate more as a cue to nectar content, not as a preference in itself.

Red, pink and orange flowers' drawing

No Pesticides, Please!

If you want to be an ally to hummingbirds, get rid of that spray gun or can of weed or insect killer. If you kill the insects you regard as pests, you may be denying hummingbirds a natural food source. Further, if hummingbirds dine on nectar after chemicals are applied to plants, they ingest the poison.

It's far better to cultivate native plants with their native resistance to local insects. Please respect the web of life and let your backyard ecology develop its own rhythms. Nearly all hummingbirds need spiderwebbing to bind their nests together and glue them to a branch. If you kill off most insects, the spiders will starve and the hummingbirds' nests and young will suffer.

Let your flower garden bloom naturally, without the use of herbicides and pesticides, to keep hummingbirds (and the insects they rely on) healthy.

If there's an insect infestation in the garden, try blasting plants with a strong stream of water from the hose. If you must resort to stronger measures, use insecticidal soap, dormant oils or other natural approaches, if you want to maintain healthy birds and healthy habitat.

power probably is primarily due to these colors' high visibility against green foliage. And, over time, hummingbirds have learned that red and orange flowers are usually the richest sources of nectar. Next they'll probe purple, blue and yellow blossoms for nectar. Last choice is white, but there are some white flowers that do attract hummingbirds. On average, a hummingbird may visit more than 1,500 flowers a day for nectar to fuel its active lifestyle.

Opposite: Hummingbirds love closely spaced flowers that make it easy to flit efficiently from bloom to bloom. In this case, honeysuckle is the offering. Note the nearby feeder.

Hummingbird Flowers

Quite a few plants have evolved to attract hummingbirds—and only hummingbirds—to drink their nectar and carry off pollen. The way the little birds and wild flowers have adapted to each other's needs is called co-evolution. There are some 150 species of blooming plants that are known as hummingbird flowers, with features that seem to have evolved specifically to appeal to hummingbirds. A hummingbird flower generally is a perennial, allowing birds to count on its presence year after year. It has a red, trumpet-shaped bloom, with space enough between flowers that a hummingbird's wings can beat freely as it hovers. It must also offer a rich supply of nectar and, of course, bloom during the day. Hummingbirds seem to prefer plants with many small flowers that bloom over a long period of time, as opposed to those with only a few, large blooms that fade quickly and drop.

Some examples of hummingbird flowers include fuchsias (*Fuchsia* spp.), columbines (*Aquilegia* spp.), cardinal flower (*Lobelia cardinalis*), ocotillo (*Fouquieria splendens*) and penstemon (*Penstemon* spp).

A hummingbird flower says "welcome" to hummingbirds and "keep out!" to insects. These flowers share several design features that serve as insect deterrents. For one, they usually have little or no fragrance. Scent is a powerful insect attractant but wasted on birds, with their poorly developed sense of smell. Also, hummingbird flowers offer no place for insects to land or perch. This makes them inhospitable to all but the one family

The best hummingbird flowers bloom for a long period of time. These red penstemon flowers do the job perfectly.

Cardinal flower is a tried, true and effective hummingbird favorite. You can't go wrong growing plenty of *Lobelia*.

A Sweet Reward

Here's what plants are saying to hummingbirds: "If you'll take this pollen over to that plant over there, you can have a sip of some nice, sweet liquid." Nectar has only one purpose—as a reward for transferring pollen. Nectar-producing cells within a plant make the sugar, then dump it inside the flower, where it mixes with water. As a hummingbird probes for nectar, it picks up pollen on its beak or head.

The flowers that draw hummingbirds back for more have a nectar concentration that is about 20 to 25 percent sugar (about twice as sweet as the average soft drink). In contrast, insects seem to prefer a much sweeter solution, 40 percent sugar or more. So the flowers that entice hummingbirds probably aren't very appealing to insects' "sweet tooth."

Make hummingbird nectar for feeders in a 1:4 ratio (see page 156), to replicate the 20 percent sugar concentration in the nectar from hummingbirds' favorite plants.

of birds perfectly equipped to hover while feeding. Finally, the color red is a beacon to hummingbirds but is lost on insects, since most insects can't see colors at the red end of the spectrum. In fact, many hummingbird flowers have evolved to such dependency on the little birds that they couldn't reproduce without them.

Big Eaters

A researcher studying a single Costa's hummingbird (*Calypte costae*) counted 42 feeding trips over six-and-one-half hours, with the bird visiting a total of 1,300 flowers. A bird like a ruby-throated hummingbird (*Archilochus colubris*) needs about 0.07 ounces of sugar a day, which might require probing 2,000 flowers for nectar. A hummingbird may easily consume half its weight in nectar and insects each day. (In contrast, we humans tend to consume about 1 percent of our weight in food a day.) The hummingbirds' fast metabolism converts sugar to energy very quickly, so within 15 minutes or so they must go back for more. It's been said that being a hummingbird is like driving a car with a one-gallon gas tank.

Nectar Is the Prize

Nectar is a plant's reward for birds and insects that perform pollination services. Hummingbirds do this unknowingly, picking up pollen on their heads or beaks as they lap up nectar, then fertilizing a nearby plant of the same species when they next stop to drink. Pollinators like hummingbirds are vital links in the chain of healthy plant communities.

Why should a plant care whether it's a bird or an insect carrying its pollen? Why welcome hummingbirds but slam the door on bees and beetles? Plants have "learned" that warm-blooded birds are more reliable pollinators. Birds are active on cold and wet days, when cold-blooded insects must conserve their energies, and birds travel farther and more widely. Thus, birds are a better guarantee of future plant generations than insects are.

If you'd like to tempt hummingbirds to stay in your area to feed and nest, you'll need to provide a steady succession of blooming plants so the birds won't need to leave the area in search of food. Springtime blooms serve to attract migrating hummingbirds and help replenish body fat lost during their long journeys. Summer blooms are an important food source for mother birds rushing to feed themselves and their hungry twins. As the seasons progress, hummingbirds are drawn to fall-blooming plants to help put on fat for their southbound migration.

Plan for a steady progression of blooms all summer long, to keep hummingbirds coming. Shown: columbines.

Opposite: This female ruby-throated hummingbird really gets her head into a fuchsia flower. When she goes to the next flower, and the next one after that, the pollen on her beak and head will go with her, fertilizing those blossoms.

One of the keys to enjoyable, exciting hummingbird viewing is placing flowers and feeders close to where you and other observers will be.

Creating Habitat

A viable habitat for a hummingbird must have four vital elements:

- food
- water
- cover
- nesting sites

Luckily, creating hummingbird habitat that has each of these elements doesn't require a great deal of time, effort or expense.

Food: Flower nectar is a natural food, but most hummingbirds aren't very particular about the source of their sugary drink. Hang nectar feeders in your garden to supplement your blooming plants (see Chapter 9). Insects are another important food source, so try not to discourage the aphids, fruit flies, leafhoppers, spiders and other invertebrates that visit your yard and garden.

Water: Hummingbirds derive a great deal of liquid from nectar, but they're still little demons for water, especially running water. They're always looking for a place to wash nectar off feathers and beaks. If you have a fountain or mister in your birdbath, hummingbirds will take notice. A pond or falling water stream with a shallow area is good, too. Hummingbirds love to zip through falling water, even if it's merely the spray from a garden hose.

Cover: Aim for the "hop, skip and jump" look in landscaping. This means having trees for birds to "hop" into for resting and nesting; mid-level vegetation they can "skip" down to for resting and perching; and then "jump" to low shrubs and plants that offer food. All birds, not just hummingbirds, appreciate this

Bathing Birds

Hummingbirds have a strong attraction to water. Even though nectar provides a great deal of liquid, the little birds do drink water from time to time and are avid bathers. They frequently need to clean sticky sugar solution from their feathers and beaks. But because they're so small, they seldom will use a conventional birdbath for a good splash —the water is usually too deep for safety. Falling water and spraying water are their preferred modes of bathing, so attractive birdbaths offer a fountain or mist attachment. Another good attractant is a birdbath with water spilling over the edge—hummingbirds will perch on the lip to bathe. Consider how hummingbirds frequently bathe in the wild: They find plant leaves covered with dew or raindrops and "surf" across the surface. If you can rig up a spray of water onto a small tree or a shrub, hummingbirds may appear from miles around.

Water brings all kinds of birds—including hummingbirds—to the garden. Since hummingbirds prefer showers over baths, it's worth the extra effort to provide a drip or flow, as with this simple setup.

kind of tiered approach. Because it approximates what they find in the wild, it's much more successful in attracting birds than planting a single tree surrounded by green grass.

A dense thicket of shrubs is a surefire way to appeal to hummingbirds and songbirds alike. They like being able to flit in and out through the branches and appreciate being able to see the approach of predators without being observed themselves.

(If you haven't heard it before, here's the skinny on lawns—they look like a barren desert to birds. Since most turf grasses are not native plants, they don't attract native insects and they provide nothing in the way of food or shelter for birds. The less lawn you have, the better for birds and the better for the environment, since turf grasses require heavy doses of fertilizer and weed-control chemicals to thrive.)

For all their speed and agility, hummingbirds spend a great deal of time perching, with up to 80 percent of each day spent resting on a twig or branch. While perching, they're surveying their territory, preening, watching for insects to eat and intruders to chase and just plain resting. Also, by perching conspicuously, males are sending a message to other males: "This territory is taken." For all these uses, they need a leafless branch or twig located high enough to provide a good view and far enough from feeders and flowers (say, 15 feet) to provide a vantage point. If you don't have naturally occurring perches in your backyard, you can create one or more by "planting" a dead branch or metal pole in the ground. Feeding makes up only a small portion of a hummingbird's day, so the hospitable garden will provide one or more perches.

Nesting: There are times when hummingbirds choose to be inconspicuous. This is true

Because we only see them buzzing about, it's easy to think that hummingbirds don't rest. In reality, the birds spend up to 80 percent of each day perched on a twig or branch. Your hummingbird garden needs to provide such resting places. Pictured: a male broad-tail.

for nesting females, sleeping birds and hummingbirds dodging a predator. For these kinds of activities, the birds need dense vegetation some distance from human disturbance. Evergreen trees and shrubs are important resting and nesting sites. If your yard currently lacks evergreens, try to accommodate several shrubs and trees at the back of your property and/or around the edges.

Evergeens, leafy deciduous shrubs and small trees all provide important hummingbird nesting cover. Here, a female ruby-throat prepares to add a piece of lichen to her nest to help camouflage it.

Hummingbird Predators

Even though hummingbirds are fast and agile, they don't always come out ahead in confrontations with larger species. They're most vulnerable while perched or hovering, and cats take a toll at such times. You can help hummingbirds avoid cats by hanging feeders higher than a cat can leap and away from vegetation where a cat can lurk.

There are reports of roadrunners snapping up hummingbirds at nectar feeders, and the rare oriole has been known to attack a hummingbird if the two compete at a nectar feeder. Praying mantises and the occasional frog can snatch a small hummingbird, while squirrels and snakes prey on eggs and chicks.

Most of these attacks are opportunistic, meaning that they resulted from chance encounters. Hummingbirds have few natural enemies, which may account for their innate curiosity and fearlessness.

Don't kid yourself into thinking cats can't kill hummingbirds. As with other feeders, hang your hummingbird feeders higher than a cat can leap, and away from spots were cats can lurk.

More Than Flowers

As you can see, it takes more than red flowers to get hummingbirds to stop, look around and decide to set up housekeeping. It takes good habitat to maintain hummingbirds, but their requirements aren't difficult to meet. Get them to stop once and they'll almost surely be back: Hummingbirds seem to have prodigious memories, and they often return to the same backyard, mountain streamside or desert bush each year. Even more impressive, they come back on nearly the same date, year after year.

Your garden should announce, "Hummingbird café, open for business." In the chapters that follow, we'll give you specific suggestions keyed to your area's climate and conditions.

With an array of bloom shapes, colors and sizes, this garden doesn't just ask for a hummingbird's attention, it shouts for it. Cannas and zinnias fill the foreground here.

Which of the "Big 8" Hummingbirds to Look for in the Spring in Your Area:

Ruby-Throated Hummingbird *(Archilochus colubris)*—begins arriving along the Gulf Coast in late February, reaches northern latitudes from Minnesota to Massachusetts by May 1; southern Canada, from Alberta to the Maritime Provinces, by mid- to late May.

Black-Chinned Hummingbird *(Archilochus alexandri)*—migrates in to southeastern Texas, southern Arizona and California in early March; moves through Colorado, Utah and Oregon by early May; reaches British Columbia by mid-May.

Anna's Hummingbird *(Calypte anna)*—a year-round resident along the Pacific Coast and inland through southern Arizona to Texas.

Costa's Hummingbird *(Calypte costae)*—year-round in southern California to south-central Arizona; some birds begin moving northward in January and February.

Calliope Hummingbird *(Stellula calliope)*—arrives in southern California in March, reaches Washington and British Columbia in May.

Broad-Tailed Hummingbird *(Selasphorus platycercus)*—arrives in the Southwest in late February; by third week in May, reaches Montana, Idaho and southern Washington.

Rufous Hummingbird *(Selasphorus rufus)*—arrives in Arizona in February, then migrates up the Pacific Coast in short bursts; reaches Washington in early March and southern Alaska by late May.

Allen's Hummingbird *(Selasphorus sasin)*—first birds arrive along Pacific Coast in January, with migration continuing into March. Some birds live year-round on southern California coast.

Hummingbirds in Winter

Don't worry about leaving your hummingbird feeders up too long. There's a persistent rumor that a nectar feeder left hanging in the fall might keep birds from migrating, luring them to perish in cold weather. But that simply isn't true. Hummingbirds, like all migratory birds, have a strong internal clock that determines their migration season. It takes external cues, such as shorter day length, to provide the final push to depart. Having food available isn't enough to stop a healthy bird from migrating. In fact, leaving your feeders hanging an extra couple weeks in the fall may provide a life-saving drink to stragglers. (See Chapter 9.)

Speaking of hummingbirds in winter, bird banders in the southeastern United States are no longer surprised when Western hummingbirds show up in their nets. The rufous hummingbird is the champion vagabond, appearing with regularity in southern Louisiana and points east in winter. There are other vagrant hummingbirds, as well: Black-chinned and calliope hummingbirds have been reported far to the east of their normal ranges in winter, as have eight other species. Researchers are not entirely clear about what motivates these birds to set off on a fly-about. But one thing we do know: Feeders left up late into the fall may provide a vital meal to birds far from their home turf.

4
Hummingbirds and Your Garden

Let a man plant a flower garden almost anywhere from Canada to Argentina and Chile, in the lowlands or mountains, amid humid forests or in irrigated deserts, and before long his bright blossoms will be visited by a tiny, glittering creature that hovers before them with wings vibrated into twin halos while it sucks their sweet nectar.

Ornithologist Alexander F. Skutch, in *The Life of the Hummingbird*

Hummingbird Blooms

Take a look at a successful hummingbird garden and you'll invariably find a gardener who falls into one of two camps. Some of us plant gardens whose sole purpose is to attract hummingbirds—these "nectar farmers" may be more interested in the birds than the blooms. Others of us are gardeners first and foremost and see it as an added benefit if our plantings happen to attract hummingbirds.

Whether you count yourself in the first group or the second, we can all take several easy steps to increase our chances for a hummingbird visit. And, with the cooperation of geography and habitat, you might even earn the ultimate accolade: a female hummingbird building her nest on or near your property.

A classic hummingbird garden is relaxed and free flowing, with plenty of blossoms for hummers to feed at, good security cover to hide in, thick places in which to nest, and water to bathe in and drink.

Most of the hummingbirds that are found in the United States and southern and western Canada are migrants, visiting for a fairly brief time to breed and raise their young before heading back to winter homes in the tropics. If we want to enjoy hummingbirds in our backyards, we've got to make sure they notice our gardens and feeders as they dash through, and we need to entice them to linger. So, as a first step, we can all benefit from taking a good, hard look at our yards and gardens. Are we good hosts, providing everything a hummingbird needs to feel at home? To answer this question, we need to try to think like a hummingbird.

Look around your "back 40" and see if you're offering what a tiny, high-energy bird needs. Even if you've made your yard and garden hospitable to songbirds, with feeders, birdbath and birdhouses, you may need to work a bit harder to attract hummingbirds. After all, they're very different from songbirds and have different requirements.

Having a birdbath is good, and adding a fountain or mister is even better. A stand of tall evergreens toward the back provides good cover and even nesting places. Other evergreen shrubs placed around your property give hummingbirds places to "bounce" around without much exposure to predators. A profusely flowering

Garden Basics

Creating good habitat for hummingbirds isn't difficult, but it's not something that happens overnight, either. Here are some tips for maximizing what you already have and adding to it over time:

- Preserve existing vegetation, especially shrubs and trees, which provide food and cover, especially if they're native plants.

- Choose plants that are suited to your property: shade-tolerant plants for shady areas, erosion-control plants for slopes, etc.

- Use the repetition principle and plant several plants of each kind. This is more pleasing to the eye and to wildlife.

- Keep the importance of cover and shelter in mind: Allow shrubs and vines to grow naturally and fill in over time.

- Think in terms of layers—groundcover, shrub, understory and canopy—to attract the greatest diversity of wild things.

- Take your time and work on one section or one bed at a time. Learn by trial and error what plants are most pleasing to hummingbirds in your area and which fit best with local climate conditions.

- Be sure to have fun. After all, gardening shouldn't be a chore, but should add to our pleasure in being outdoors. And gardening to attract birds is a great combination of two of our most popular leisure-time activities.

vine draped over a fence or other structure is doubly appreciated. It offers blooms for food and foliage for lurking and perching. And then there's the whole realm of flowering plants. We have so many choices and so many ways to please those little palates, it can sometimes seem almost overwhelming.

Hummingbirds love low-key gardens that lean toward the wild side. Note this feeder's proximity to a window, where human viewers can enjoy the show.

Start Slow

If you're new to hummingbird gardening, it's probably best to begin slowly. Start out with three or four blooming plants your first gardening season. Add a few more as times goes on and you see what works in your climate and what successfully attracts hummingbirds.

The traditionally landscaped property, featuring a groomed lawn, neatly kept flower beds and sheared shrubs, looks completely foreign to migrating hummingbirds. They've just come from tropical regions, where the plant world is a burgeoning riot of green interspersed with blooms of every hue. Wild creatures like nature on the wild side. In fact, if you could poll the hummingbirds (and other birds) in your area, they'd surely all say, "Get rid of all that grass, let those shrubs grow every which way and give us big splashes of color!"

Our whole concept of landscaping is changing as more and more gardeners plant with wildlife in mind. Dedicated gardeners are researching which flowers, trees and shrubs grow naturally in their area, and which offer the optimum food and shelter to birds and other animals. If we can't find what we want at our local garden stores, we're looking through catalogs and Internet sites for appropriate seeds and plants. Fortunately, more and more garden centers are expanding their perennial sections to include native plants. Specialty nurseries devoted entirely to natives are springing up in many areas as well.

Return of the Natives

Why all this talk about native plants? Natives make a good first choice because returning hummingbirds immediately recognize them. It's like putting out that special cocktail mix when Uncle Ed is coming to visit. Because most hummingbirds live and nest in the wild, the plants they respond to quickly are the ones that grow naturally in a region.

Over many millennia, native plants have adapted to local conditions. They thrive in the temperature, soil conditions and precipitation found in their particular region. In the Western mountains, hummingbirds are attracted by native Indian paintbrushes

(*Castilleja* spp.) and penstemons (*Penstemon* spp.). In the East, bee balm (*Monarda* spp.) and trumpet creeper (*Campsis radicans*) bring in the birds, while in the Southwest, salvias (*Salvia* spp.) and desert honeysuckle (*Anisacanthus thurberi*) do the job. Native plants in bloom will be the first to catch a hummingbird's eye, since

Hummingbirds will usually come to native plants before visiting exotics. So build the base of your hummingbird garden around natives such as Indian paintbrush, pictured.

In desert or other country of the West, ocotillo (pictured) is a hummingbird favorite. Its color, flower shape and abundant nectar are perfect for hummers.

they know these flowers and how much nectar they provide. It's akin to seeing a familiar motel sign during a long road trip. (See region-specific plant suggestions in the chapters that follow.)

The great thing about natives is that they're tough and resilient. After they become established, they need very little care, unlike most other plants available at the garden store. Natives don't require fertilizers or pesticides, and they need very little supplemental water. Over eons, they've learned to develop coping mechanisms for the weather and defenses against insect pests. So planting natives means less work for you—less watering, less fertilizing, no pesticides—and a smaller "footprint" on the environment.

More and more of us are seeing that the choices we make every day in our homes and gardens have an impact on everything around us, including air and water quality and the health and safety of ourselves and our wildlife visitors. Plant natives, and you'll have more time to enjoy your gardens and the birds they attract and the comfort of knowing your gardening practices aren't harming your guests.

Opposite: Desert honeysuckle (*Anisacanthus thurberi*) is another good hummingbird plant for the arid West.

Invisible Nests

If you've ever seen a hummingbird nest, count yourself lucky. Female hummingbirds are so good at hiding and camouflaging these small structures that few people ever see them.

Most are the size of a walnut shell half, barely two inches across and shaped like a tiny cup. They're built from soft grasses, moss and plant fibers. In most cases, the female hummingbird attaches moss, lichen or bark bits to the exterior, which makes her nest blend in perfectly with the branch it's built on.

Nests are knit together and attached to branches with spider silk, an important ingredient for hummingbird architects. The female, who handles the chores of nest building, brooding and raising the young all by herself, lays two tiny eggs the size of navy beans. As the young birds grow, the loose weave of the nest and the "give" of the spider silk allow the nest to expand around them.

Many hummingbirds build their nests on tree branches near streams and rivers, and they're so well camouflaged they pass for a knot in the wood.

Checks and Balances

Nonnative plants lack all the checks and balances that have developed over the ages to maintain a healthy ecosystem. They lack the insect controls and climatic cues that keep our native vegetation in line. Without such controls, they often become invasive, crowding out valuable native plants and the beneficial insects and other organisms that birds rely on.

Here's one example: In many areas of the continent, the fast-growing, nonnative common buckthorn (*Rhamnus cathartica*) was a popular shrub and hedge choice in the 1950s and 1960s. As songbirds spread the seed, buckthorn exploded out of backyards into parks, vacant lots and wild areas. Buckthorn crowds out everything else and quickly becomes its own monoculture. In Minnesota, where I live, parks and public lands and even the banks of the Mississippi River are infested with this invasive plant. In fact, the understory of most woodlands and forests in and near cities is now buckthorn. It will take years of backbreaking effort to eradicate it, if it's even possible to do so. The best solution is not to plant greedy, uncontrolled vegetation like this in the first place.

Birds Arrive Before Blooms

In many parts of the country, native plants alone will not be sufficient to attract hummingbirds, especially in the early spring, since savvy native plants wait until the weather is

fairly clement before coming into bloom. But many hummingbirds begin migrating northward before that time. That's certainly true in my area, within U.S.D.A. Hardiness Zone 4, where very little other than bleeding heart (*Dicentra* spp.) is in bloom around May 1, when the first ruby-throated hummingbirds (*Archilochus colubris*) begin arriving, hungry for some quick energy.

In previous years, I've had very little luck in getting any ruby-throats to slow down and spend some time in my yard. I now see the error of my ways. Most years, I've waited until I see that first hummingbird before dashing around, mixing up sugar water, finding and filling feeders and hanging them outdoors. This usually occurs in late April, and by then it's already too late; the birds familiar with this specific area have scouted it out, found it deficient and moved on.

From now on, things will be different. With that May 1 arrival date in mind, I'll plan to fill and hang those feeders in mid-April, providing a two-week window for early hummingbirds. On cold nights, I'll bring the feeders indoors, then place them back outdoors as the sun comes up.

Opposite: Nonnative plants have their place in the hummingbird garden—especially in spring, when their early blooms can attract the first returning migrants. Bleeding heart (*Dicentra spectabilis*, shown) is one such plant.

Old Age

Even though hummingbirds live fast-paced lives with mind-boggling heart rates and high-velocity metabolisms, burnout doesn't seem to be a problem. Actually, the tiny birds are surprisingly long-lived. A hummingbird that survives its first year has a good chance to live another four, with five years being the average life span for many species. Banded birds provide good information about longevity, with bird banders sometimes finding birds eight and nine years old, and even the rare 12-year-old in their nets. Birds raised in captivity in zoos and aviaries live longer, with up to 10 or 12 years being the average.

(With little in the way of fat reserves, hummingbirds need to replenish their energy stores quickly after a long, cold night.) I'm going to hang a basket of red-flowering blooms and plug in the birdbath fountain. And maybe, just maybe, some ruby-throats will learn to love it in my garden.

A Bright Spot of Color

If you feel equally inspired and haven't previously had much luck in drawing in hummingbirds, try planting a bed with bright blooming annuals, select hanging baskets with nectar-rich flowers (fuchsias work wonders) and fill window boxes or containers with red, orange and pink blooms. Be sure to place your nectar feeders out early, two weeks before you expect the first birds in your area (see chapters that follow for average arrival dates).

Emphasizing plants native to your area doesn't need to mean excluding plants from elsewhere. Many tropical plants (which the birds may recognize from their winter homes) may enjoy a shorter growing season in temperate climates but are popular with hummingbirds. Go ahead and plant a shrimp plant (*Justicia brandegeeana*) if it grows in your zone, but let's always balance hummingbird preferences with the needs of the environment. Keeping that balance in mind makes the wildly invasive Japanese honeysuckle (*Lonicera japonica*) a poor choice for any garden. Hummingbirds love the flowers, but the plant quickly takes over and can spread throughout the neighborhood.

Annuals make very good choices for hummingbird gardens as well. They're bright and long-blooming, and many are good nectar sources. Think of the many salvias (*Salvia* spp.), that grow as annuals in most areas, and cleome (*Cleome* spp.), impatiens (*Impatiens* spp.) and zinnias (*Zinnia* spp.). However, savvy hummingbird gardeners often place more emphasis on perennials. Once they become established, perennials require little care and return year after year, saving you both time and money.

Eye-Catching Red

Most people are aware of hummingbirds' affinity for the color red. They're very curious little birds, and they'll investigate just about anything with a red tone, including flowers, hanging feeders, human hats and clothing and even traffic signs. It's not that hummingbirds see red more clearly than other colors. But red and orange flowers contrast with the green leaves surrounding them, beckoning like beacons to birds new to your backyard. Not every red blossom is a good source of nectar, but hummingbirds have learned, through trial and error, that many red flowers are worth a stop.

Any color is good color in a hummingbird garden, but red is still the best. Shown here: penstemon.

Opposite: Annuals have their place in a good hummingbird garden. Here are cosmos, verbena, zinnia, salvia and snapdragon. What hummingbird could resist this explosion of blooms?

Cat Control!

One other vital point: Now that you've done all you can to attract hummingbirds, are you exposing them to danger in the form of the domestic cat? Hummingbirds hovering at flowers, bathing in a birdbath fountain or resting on a limb are extremely vulnerable to cat attacks. Please keep your own felines indoors and talk to any neighbors with free-roaming cats. If cats do enter your garden, you can equip your nectar feeder poles with squirrel guards to keep cats from leaping to catch hummingbirds. You also could place chicken wire or some other fencing material around the birdbath and around the base of trees and shrubs.

We each have a responsibility to keep our whirring guests safe during their visits. Because they're fearless and curious, hummingbirds have few defenses against predators, other than beating a speedy retreat, which sometimes is not enough when faced with a cunning cat.

They have several other preferences, as well. Hummingbirds seem to prefer flowers with long, narrow tubes. Their long, slim beaks make an easy job of probing for nectar and small insects, and their grooved tongues quickly lap up both the sweet syrup and insects. Nectar is their reward for picking up pollen and transferring it to another plant. (In fact, some hummingbirds are so covered with pollen after a busy feeding session that they could be called "yellow-throated" or "yellow-crowned" hummingbirds.)

Successful hummingbird gardeners report that it's a good strategy to plant flowers in clumps and spread out the clumps. Certainly, a profusion of red-blooming plants in one corner of the garden has high hummingbird visibility. However, a bully hummingbird can easily take over and fight off all competitors for this dining oasis. Better to spread the blooms around, with a red clump here and a red and orange clump there, so several hummingbirds can feed at once.

Continuous Bloom

One other key point: Keep bloom succession in mind. As the flowers of one plant begin to fade, another should be coming into full bloom, from spring through fall, to continue to draw in hummingbirds. Before buying a plant, check its blooming season and try to have a range of early-, middle- and late-blooming plants in your garden.

Flowers mean food, but don't forget about hummingbirds' need for cover and shelter—elements that some feel may be even more important than blooming plants. Having a stand of dense shrubs, some evergreen trees or bushes and some thick vines creates a comfort zone for hummingbirds. They need safe places that they can fly to whenever they feel the need (for example, if a cat is roaming the yard). And they need perches—if there's no place to perch, hummingbirds simply won't settle in. After all, eating consumes 20 percent of each day, but perching makes up the other 80 percent.

On page 82, you'll find a list of plant families and some examples of plants in those families that make excellent choices as nectar sources for a hummingbird garden. Please keep in mind that not all will thrive in every region, but within these families, there surely will be three or more plants that will help make your garden a hummingbird hot spot.

Hummingbirds love bee balm (*Monarda*) flowers, putting to rest the idea that only deep, trumpet-shaped flowers attract hummers. The birds want nectar, and bee balm offers plenty of it.

The Hummingbird Top Ten

The plants on the list below may either be perennials or annuals and native or exotics, depending on whether they grow in your area naturally. Choose from this list and you will have blooms that attract hummingbirds.

Mint Family: Salvias from Texas Sage (*Salvia coccinea*) to Bee Balm (*Monarda didyma*)

Honeysuckles: including Trumpet Honeysuckle (*Lonicera sempervirens*) and Orange Honeysuckle (*L. ciliosa*)

Penstemons: from Firecracker Penstemon (*P. eatonii*) to Pineleaf Penstemon (*P. pinifolius*)

Mallows: choose Turk's Cap (*Malvaviscus arboreus* var. 'drummondii') or Flowering Maple (*Abutilon pictus*)

Morning Glories: Red Morning Glory (*Ipomora coccinea*) or Bush Morning Glory (*I. leptophylla*)

Columbines: choose red and yellow species, such as Yellow Columbine (*Aquilegia chrysantha*) and Wild Columbine (*A. canadensis*)

Lobelias: select Cardinal Flower (*Lobelia cardinalis*) or Blue Cardinal Flower (*L. siphilitica*)

Bignonias: Trumpet Creeper (*Campsis radicans*) is a good choice, as is Desert Willow (*Chilopsis linearis*)

Evening Primrose Family: from White Fireweed (*Epilobium angustifolium*) to California Fuchsia (*Zauschneria californica*)

Acanthuses: from Chuparosa (*Justicia californica*) to Shrimp Plant (*J. brandegeeana*)

The Basic Formula

To recap the hummingbird basics: Plant flowers that come into bloom at staggered times so you'll have a continuous blooming schedule. In most plant hardiness zones, hang baskets of blooms in early spring, and in all areas, add nectar feeders to supplement them. Plant fast-growing annuals and a variety of perennials for summer and try to have a late-blooming vine for summer and fall.

All the honeysuckles attract hummingbirds. Shown here is orange honeysuckle, *Lonicera ciliosa*.

Even if hummingbirds skip over your yard on the way to nesting areas, they'll probably be back in the fall. Keep in mind that fall migration starts early for most hummingbirds, as early as late July and early August. Their numbers are highest at this time of year, with the recently fledged young birds joining the migratory stream. Catch their eyes early, feed them through summer if you have them, then fatten them up for the long trip to the tropics. That's the basic formula, and it's easy to do.

For some more ideas for what to plant and when various plants bloom, visit an arboretum in your area, a nature center or public hummingbird gardens.

Many varieties of columbine will bring hummingbirds to your garden.

Hummingbird Trees and Shrubs

Apple and Crabapple trees (*Malus* spp.)

Azalea (*Rhododendron* spp.)

Butterfly Bush (*Buddleia* spp.)

Citrus trees (*Citrus* spp.)

Flowering Currants (*Ribes* spp.)

Flowering Quince (*Chaenomeles* spp.)

Lilac (*Syringa* spp.)

Manzanita (*Arctostaphylos* spp.)

Mimosa (*Albizia julibrissin*)

Red Buckeye (*Aesculus pavia*)

Weigela (*Weigela* spp.)

Hummingbird Vines

Trumpet Creeper (*Campsis radicans*)

Red Morning Glory (*Ipomoea coccinea*)

Cardinal Climber (*Ipomoea* x 'multifida')

Trumpet Honeysuckle (*Lonicera sempervirens*)

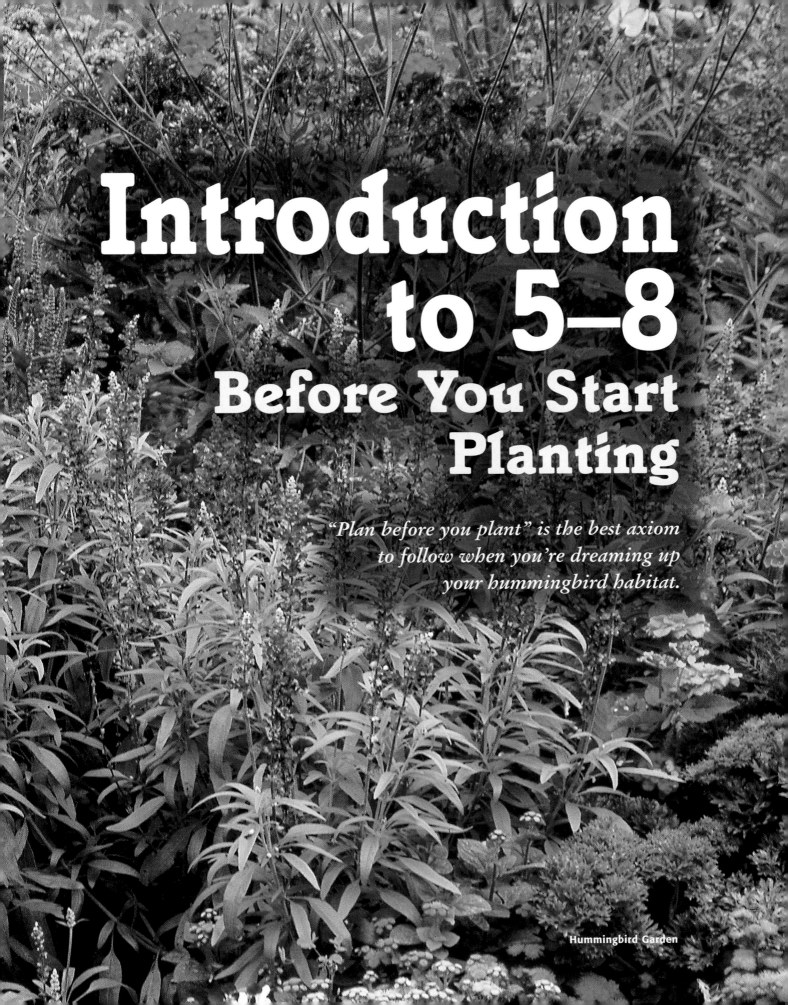

Introduction to 5–8
Before You Start Planting

"Plan before you plant" is the best axiom to follow when you're dreaming up your hummingbird habitat.

Hummingbird Garden

It's important to keep in mind that every part of the United States and southern and western Canada has at least one hummingbird species flying over it at some time during the year. This means that if you keep hummingbirds in mind as you plan and plant your garden, you can almost count on being rewarded with visits by vibrant, darting little birds, particularly during spring and fall migration.

As we've seen, hummingbirds (like all birds) have four basic needs in order to live and breed successfully. These include food (in the form of nectar-producing flowers and small insects, supplemented by feeders), water (especially in the form of a mist or fountain), spots for shelter (in thick vines and shrubs) and nesting areas (in shrubs, vines and trees). If your yard and garden feature all four of these, you've enhanced your chances for attracting hummingbirds.

If you're new to gardening and/or new to gardening to attract hummingbirds, don't exhaust yourself or your budget by trying to create the perfect garden all at once. Make changes gradually, over several planting seasons. Start by selecting three to five flowering plants and group several of each kind together for a massed effect. Next, add a flowering vine, then a fountain or mister to the birdbath and hang a nectar feeder nearby. If there are few shrubs or trees in your yard or neighborhood, draft a plan for introducing these elements into your landscape in increments. Especially in areas

Flowers attract the birds, such as this female ruby-throat, while feeders pull the birds where you want them for viewing.

Plenty of shrubs, varying bloom colors and sizes, and water combine to make gardens that are beautiful to hummingbirds as well as to your senses.

to help beginners choose appropriate plants. Many plant stores and nurseries now offer native plants and expertise as well. Plants that are native to your region thrive on the rainfall, soil and season length found locally. And, an added bonus, they're the plants hummingbirds recognize first.

Although native plants are the best choice for the health of the birds, the environment and you, hummingbirds won't shun nonnative species. In fact, they're known to make little pigs out of

where wind is a significant climate factor, planting a windbreak greatly adds to birds' comfort.

Get on Their List

These steps will encourage migratory hummingbirds to stop by on migration. And birds that stop this year will put your garden on their list for a visit next time they're in the area. Over time, you may choose to add more plantings, varying their heights and widths for a layered look, and do some research on which native plants perform best in your area. There's a native plant society in nearly every state, eager

Work to plan a progression of blooms from spring through fall. This beautiful cottage garden in late spring features columbine, iris and foxglove.

Hummingbirds can't resist some exotic plants such as this nicotiana, which is being attended by a male ruby-throat. Put exotics in baskets, pots or other containers to keep them under control.

themselves when feeding at exotics such as Mexican cigar plant (*Cuphea micropetala*), tree tobacco (*Nicotiana glauca*) and flowering maple (*Abutilon pictum*).

On the down side, exotic plants have few natural controls and many are invasive, quickly taking over a garden and surrounding areas. If an invasive shrub or vine produces berries, songbirds will "plant" them, spreading the problem far and wide. So a few exotics are fine, but let's try to garden the way Mother Nature would. One way to keep exotics under control is to plant them in baskets or pots—they'll have a tougher time making the leap to your garden.

Some gardeners in warm areas may choose to grow a few of the plants that hummingbirds encounter on their wintering grounds in Central and South America. This strategy is generally accepted, but be aware that these exotics probably won't attract the type of insects that hummingbirds are used to.

One key hummingbird-attracting strategy is to offer plants that come into flower at different times, so you'll have blooms from spring through late fall. If you need help in making sure you'll be providing blooms across the seasons, ask your local nursery, native plant society or a friend or neighbor who's a long-time gardener.

First and foremost, you need a bright, eye-catching clump of flowers for early spring. This could be a hanging basket of bright fuchsia (*Fuchsia* spp.) or a container of early blooming annuals, especially important if your region's migratory hummingbirds begin arriving before blooming season. As these first flowers fade, they should be supplanted by midsummer blooms, possibly a mixture of annuals and perennials. Then be sure to have nectar-producing blooms for the fall season as well. To hummingbirds, this kind of progressive blooming means they can count on fast food throughout their stay.

When spring is still young, hang a bright basket of blooming flowers to grab passing hummingbirds' attention. Impatiens (shown) and fuchsia do well in baskets.

Perennials and Patience

If you're emphasizing perennials—a strategy that will save you effort and money over time—you'll need to budget in some patience. Shrubs and vines often take several years to come into bloom. Fill in with bright annuals until your perennials are up to speed.

And let's keep that other important element of the hummingbird's diet in mind—insects, for protein, vitamins and minerals.

A healthy hummingbird garden will be attractive to insects, necessary both to nourish the birds and to control other, harmful insects so you needn't resort to pesticides. Start looking at insects as a solution, not as a problem: Many insects are bugbusters themselves, feasting on garden pests such as aphids.

Oh, and one more thing: Don't forget that your enjoyment is a very important part of this equation. You need to be able to see your garden to enjoy its tiny visitors, so plan your hummingbird garden for a spot that's visible from your breakfast nook, patio or wherever else you can sit and enjoy the view.

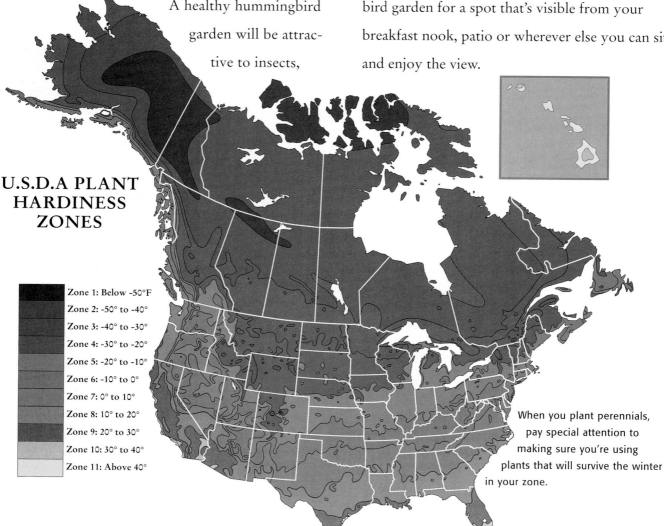

U.S.D.A PLANT HARDINESS ZONES

Zone 1: Below -50°F
Zone 2: -50° to -40°
Zone 3: -40° to -30°
Zone 4: -30° to -20°
Zone 5: -20° to -10°
Zone 6: -10° to 0°
Zone 7: 0° to 10°
Zone 8: 10° to 20°
Zone 9: 20° to 30°
Zone 10: 30° to 40°
Zone 11: Above 40°

When you plant perennials, pay special attention to making sure you're using plants that will survive the winter in your zone.

Success Factors

In the chapters that follow, we'll look at the eight ecoregions that make up the United States and southern Canada and explore some ideas for attracting hummingbirds in each one. One note of caution: We make use of the U.S.D.A. plant hardiness zone map, which divides the United States and Canada into ten zones, each of which experiences gradually colder average winter low temperatures. But there are so many other things that affect garden success, as you're no doubt aware.

Plan your hummingbird garden to thrive in your particular ecoregion. What's good for this Wyoming rufous hummingbird is different than what will work in Washington state, Minnesota, Pennsylvania or Virginia.

Where we make recommendations that generally are appropriate to an area, individual gardeners need to factor in their garden's altitude, the local precipitation pattern, average summer highs and lows, windiness and length and severity of the seasons. Here's another way to think about the complexities of garden planning: Cape Cod, Mass., Raleigh, N.C., Abilene, Texas, and Juneau, Alaska, are all cities in U.S.D.A. Hardiness Zone 7, but can you imagine finding a single plant that will thrive in all of these areas?

Then there's the precipitation issue. A plant that grows well in Texas's 20 inches of annual rainfall may not survive in another region that gets the same amount of precipitation each year, but most of it in the form of snow in winter. This is why native plants, with their built-in "drought insurance," make such good sense—they need only the amount of rainfall that naturally occurs in your region.

So go ahead and plan and plant a hummingbird garden, but keep in mind that the guidelines that follow are generalizations. Let your experience and good sense—and perhaps advice from a nursery staff or knowledgeable hummingbird gardener—guide you to specific plants for your particular area.

5

Hummingbird Gardening: Pacific Coast and Desert Southwest

U.S.D.A. Hardiness Zones 3 to 10

Black-Chinned Hummingbird, Female
At Trumpet Flower

The goal of any hummingbird garden is to offer nectar-producing flowers in all the seasons that hummingbirds are in the area. And not just any flowers will do—we need to have eye-catching, nectar-rich blooms for our hummingbird guests.

Gardens in most areas in these two regions will host hummingbirds at least during spring and fall migration. Other gardens will enjoy visitors throughout the summer, maybe a female bird nesting nearby or a territorial male who adopts your garden as his own. A few areas within these two regions even enjoy hummingbirds year-round.

Most plants bloom most vigorously in the summertime, but we'll need to make sure our hummingbird gardens also feature flowers in the spring and fall (and even in winter, in warmer areas). Whenever you're thinking of adding new plants to your garden, check their blooming times to make sure there's something in flower in each season and the garden doesn't lean too heavily toward one end of the calendar or another.

Keep in mind that hummingbirds are curious little birds that will try just about anything, not only what we traditionally think of as hummingbird flowers. Through trial and error, they learn to return to the blossoms that give them the most nectar and/or that provide nectar when little else is available. This means your garden can be as colorful as you wish—you needn't plant only red flowers for hummingbird consumption. The aptly named wooly blue curls (*Trichostema lanatum*) and the blue flowers of Cleveland sage (*Salvia clevelandii*) are good examples of non-red blooms that are exceedingly popular with hummingbirds.

Since there is such climatic variation in these two ecoregions, let's plan two basic gardens, one for the Pacific Coast and another for the Desert Southwest, making some choices from the Hummingbird Top 10 list (Chapter 4). We'll use natives wherever possible and supplement them with blooms that attract hummingbirds without harm to the local ecosystem. Hanging baskets and plants in containers are great additions to boost the brightness factor in the backyard landscape.

Please note: With such a wide range of climate conditions, elevations and precipitation within the Pacific Coast and Desert Southwest regions, the suggestions that follow are, by necessity, generalizations. Individual gardeners

Opposite: Hummingbirds love wooly blue curls (*Trichostema lanatum*), proving that red isn't the only color attractive to hummingbirds.

should customize their selections to fit their particular conditions. Please keep in mind that there are hundreds of other plants that will work well in your region. Most flowering plants produce nectar, and it's nectar that draws in hummingbirds. So your choices need be limited only by your imagination and your local ecology. You'll learn by trial and error, or advice from other "nectar farmers," what plants are favored by hummingbirds in your region.

In order to make certain that your welcome mat is rolled out all the way, keep in mind those other, vital elements of hummingbird habitat. Does your birdbath have a fountain or mister attachment for these airborne bathers? Are there perching spots available nearby in shrubs and trees? Is there cover, in the form of thick shrubbery and evergreens? These things are as important as food to hummingbirds.

Pacific Coast

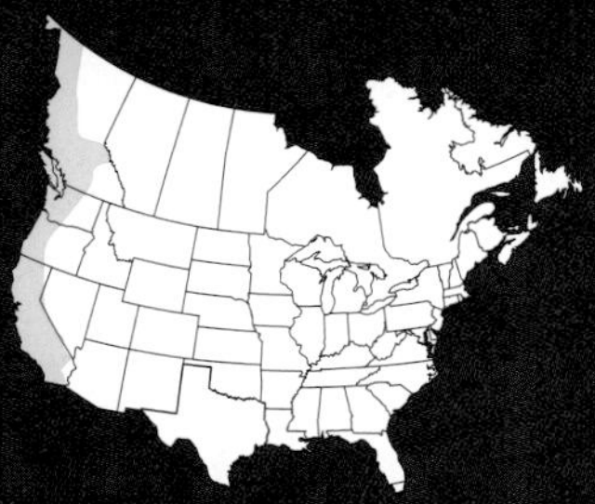

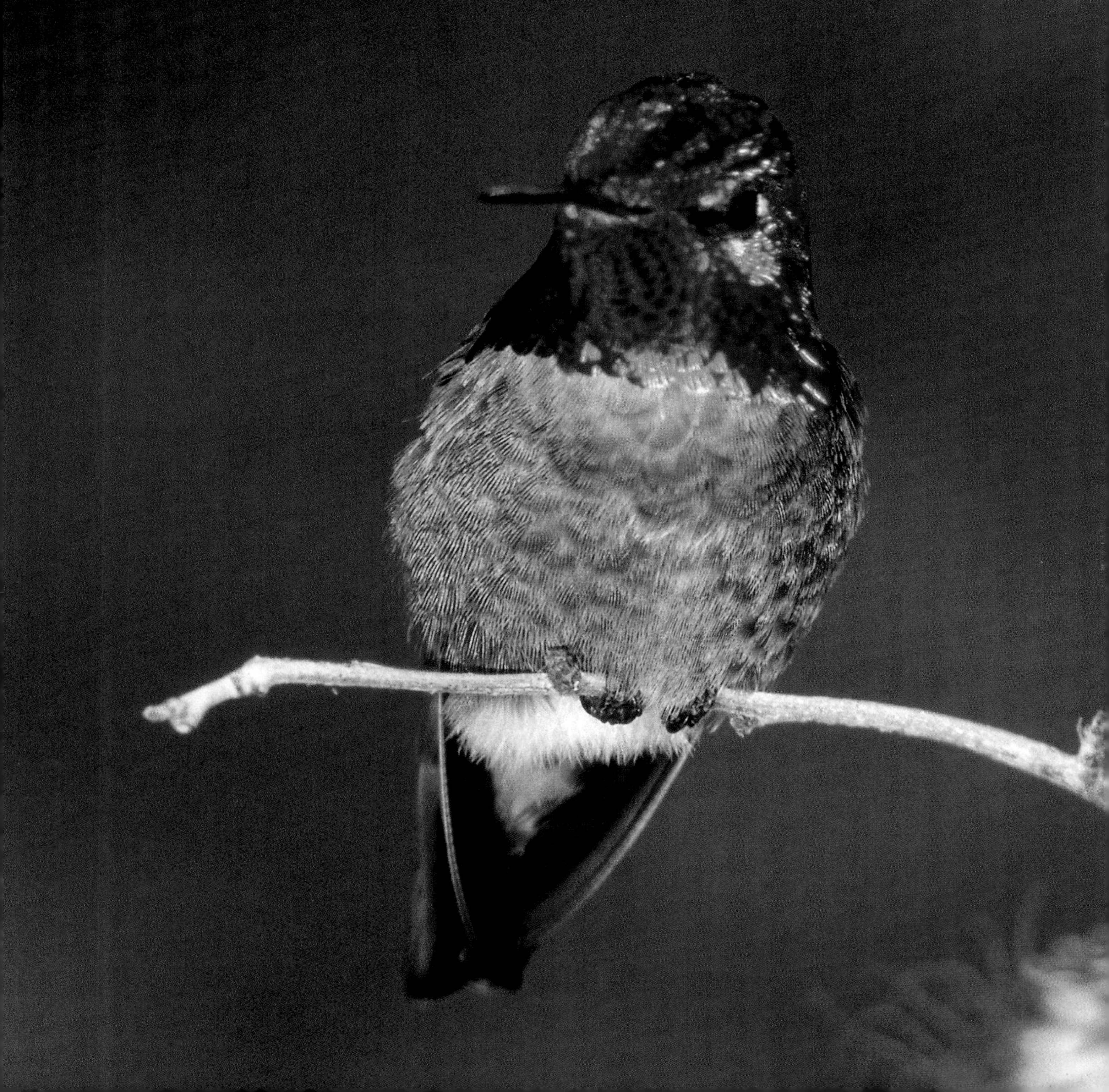

U.S.D.A. Hardiness Zones 3 to 10

Climate: From Mediterranean-like conditions in parts of southern California to desert-like heat in the major valleys, the Pacific Northwest enjoys mild, dry summers, wet winters and cool springs and falls.

Generally, six species of hummingbirds nest in this region, including the year-round Anna's hummingbird (*Calypte anna*). The five other nesting species are the Allen's (*Selasphorus sasin*), black-chinned (*Archilochus alexandri*), calliope (*Stellula calliope*), Costa's (*Calypte costae*) and the rufous (*Selasphorus rufus*).

In this region, with hummingbird migration beginning early, it's important to keep your nectar feeders filled. Because many California gardens host year-round hummingbirds, a range of nectar plants with a range of blooming times is important here. Shelter also is important to provide protection from strong seasonal winds or rainy periods. Because the climate can be very dry, birdbaths and other sources of water are a vital element of our homemade habitats. Evergreens are a great way to provide shelter and nesting sites.

Opposite: The lovely Anna's hummingbird lives in the Pacific Coast region year-round. Here, a male Anna's perches on a twig.

Manzanita offers spring flowers that attract Pacific Coast hummingbirds. Later in the year, manzanita is important for the cover and shelter it offers.

In the southern portion of the Pacific Coast region, manzanitas (*Arctostaphylos* spp.) are a good choice to provide shelter and perching spots, and many have spring flowers that attract hummingbirds. These attractive, hardy natives seem to thrive in poor soil and need almost no water once they become established.

California natives have adapted to the state's wet winters and the dry summers. In fact, they've adapted so well that they prefer dry conditions, good news for gardeners who are looking to conserve water. The crimson columbine (*Aquilegia formosa*), Indian paintbrush (*Castilleja* spp.), scarlet monkeyflower (*Mimulus cardinalis*) and penstemons (*Penstemon* spp.) are all excellent hummingbird plants. For winter bloom, add the fuchsia-flow-ered gooseberry (*Ribes speciosum*); red-hot poker plants (*Kniphofia uvaria*) attract hummingbirds in both coastal and desert areas.

Many salvias (*Salvia* spp.) make excellent choices because they're bright, full of nectar, require very little water and are magnets for hummingbirds. Plant several varieties in a group and they'll eventually form a thicket that will draw hummingbirds to feed, perch nearby and possibly nest. A late-blooming salvia, *Salvia confertiflora*, is covered with dark red flowers in autumn, just in time for hummingbirds beginning their southward migration.

Gardening challenges may include depleted clay soils in many areas, problem insects and water scarcity. Compost—and lots of it—can be the answer to enriching and aerating soil. As for insects, remember: The more you have, the more interesting your garden is to birds. Small insects that feed on small-flowered plants can be surprisingly predatory on other insects. And hummingbirds require large doses of small insects to make up the protein/vitamin/mineral portion of their diets.

Migratory hummingbirds moving northward in spring encounter a cooler, cloudier climate in the Pacific Northwest. As wet as winter often is, successful Northwestern gardeners plan for an extended warm, dry period in the summer.

Hummingbird Flowers

More than 150 plants native to North America depend exclusively on hummingbirds for pollination. They've adapted to provide nectar only to hummingbirds because hummingbirds have proved the most reliable pollinators. In a natural quid pro quo, the plants want to make sure their nectar reward goes only to hummingbirds, instead of to the myriad bugs, beetles and bees that also thrive on nectar.

As part of their exclusionary strategy, hummingbird blossoms feature long, downward-hanging tubes to be probed by long hummingbird beaks. As you read in Chapter 3, hummingbirds have a poorly developed sense of smell, so hummingbird flowers can dispense with scent. And, with their unique ability to hover, hummingbirds don't require perches in order to feed. So hummingbird flowers lack a lip or other structure that might encourage an insect to drop in. And their flowers often are red, to stand out against foliage and because hummingbirds seem to visit red blooms first.

Each region has its own native hummingbird plants. Some examples: coral bean (*Erythrina herbacea*), cardinal flower (*Lobelia cardinalis*) and chuparosa (*Justicia californica*). The deeper the flower shape, whether cup, trumpet or tube, the more room for nectar glands inside, producing more nectar for the birds—a fact the birds quickly learn.

Hardy fuchsia (*Fuchsia magellanica*), native to mountainous regions in Central and South America, does well here. Hummingbirds are fond of the flowering currant (*Ribes sanguineum*), crimson columbine (*Aquilegia formosa*) and honeysuckle shrubs such as the twinberry honeysuckle (*Lonicera involucrata*). Pine and spruce trees and shrubs provide excellent cover.

Keep native plants in mind as you design your hummingbird garden. Hummingbirds are familiar with natives and these plants act like a beacon, attracting the birds more quickly than cultivated varieties will. Native plants also support native insects, necessary both to feed hummingbirds and keep other garden pests under control. However, if a flower has nectar, hummingbirds aren't likely to check its "green card"— nectar-rich nonnatives can be welcome additions, as long as they're not invasive species just waiting to take over the neighborhood.

Salvia makes a great hummingbird plant because it is bright red, rich in nectar, easy to take care of ... and it blooms profusely.

A Hummingbird Garden for the Pacific Coast

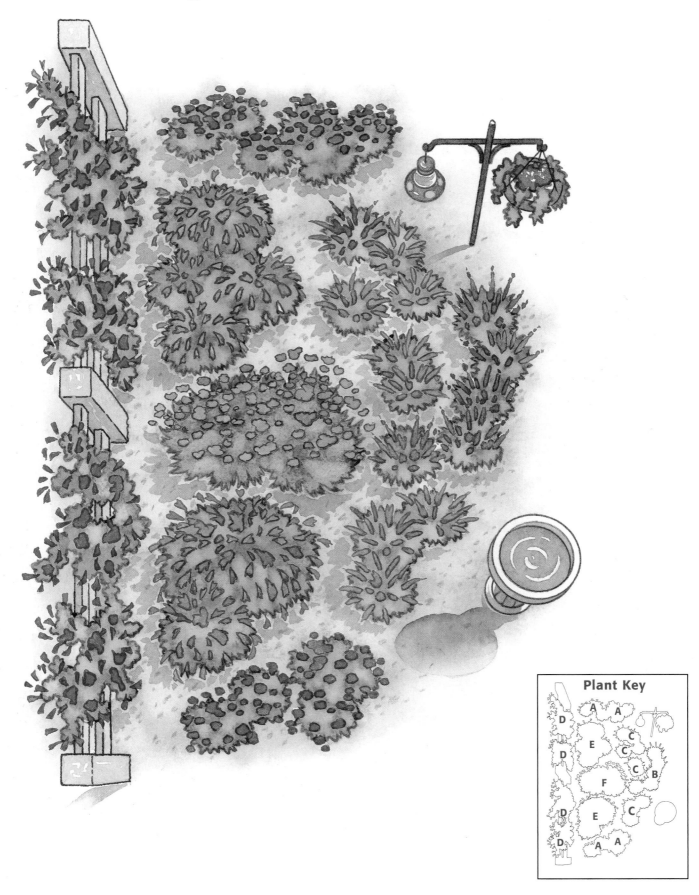

Plant Key

FLOWERS

Honeysuckles: Trumpet Honeysuckle (*Lonicera sempervirens*), spring through fall; California Honeysuckle (*L. hispidula*), summer

California Fuchsia (*Zauschneria californica*), blooms summer and fall

Bee Balm (A) (*Monarda* spp.), blooms midsummer

Cardinal Flower (B) (*Lobelia cardinalis*), blooms summer to fall

Salvias: (C) Pineapple Sage (*Salvia elegans*), blooms fall and winter; Mexican Bush Sage (*S. leucantha*), blooms summer through fall; and Anise Sage (*S. guaranitica*), blooms spring through fall

VINES

Orange Honeysuckle (*Lonicera ciliosa*), blooms in spring

Firecracker Vine (D) (*Manettia cordifolia*), blooms summer and fall

SHRUBS

Red-Flowering Currant (*Ribes sanguineum*), blooms in spring (very important for rufous hummingbirds)

Hardy Fuchsia (E) (*Fuchsia magellanica*), blooms summer to fall

Manzanita (*Arctostaphylos* spp.), blooms in spring

Cleveland Sage (F) (*S. clevelandii*), summer

To add brightness and eye-appeal to your garden, add containers of showy annuals, such as petunias (*Petunia* spp.), more salvias, snapdragons (*Antirrhinum majus*), begonias (*Begonia semperflorens*) and impatiens (*Impatiens* spp.).

There are many other good plants to consider for gardens in this region. After your basic planting plan is established, you may wish to choose from the list at right to add variety to your garden, always keeping blooming times in mind as you proceed. Something in bloom in every season is the mantra of the successful hummingbird gardener.

Some Other Plants to Consider

Crimson Columbine (*Aquilegia formosa*)

Fuschias (*F. magellanica* or *F. fulgens*)

Campion (*Silene* spp.)

Wooly Blue Curls (*Trichostema lanatum*)

Climbing Penstemon (*Keckiella cordifolius* or *Penstemon cordifolia*)

Scarlet Gilia (*Ipomopsis aggregata*)

Scarlet Monkeyflower (*Mimulus cardinalis*)

Orange Bush Monkeyflower (*Mimulus aurantiacus*)

Cigar Plant (*Cuphea* x 'David Verity')

Shrimp Plant (*Justicia brandegeeana*)

Cape Honeysuckle (*Tecomaria capensis*)

Tree Tobacco (*Nicotiana glauca*)

Lilac (*Syringa vulgaris*)

California Lilac (*Ceanothus* spp.)

Indian Paintbrush (*Castilleja* spp.)

Butterfly Bush (*Buddleia davidii*)

Japanese Flowering Quince (*Chaenomeles japonica*)

Fuchsia-Flowered Gooseberry (*Ribes speciosum*)

Salvias (*S. guaranitica, S. greggii, S. spacathea* and *S. coccinea*)

Foxglove (*Digitalis* spp.)

Hosta (*Hosta* spp.)

Island Bush Snapdragon (*Galvezia speciosa*)

Desert Southwest

> U.S.D.A. Hardiness Zones 5 to 9
>
> **Climate:** Ranges from arid, desert-like conditions at low elevations to cooler, wetter weather in the mountains.

Generally, look for nesting black-chinned (*Archilochus alexandri*) and broad-tailed hummingbirds (*Selasphorus platycercus*); Anna's hummingbirds (*Calypte anna*) and Costa's hummingbirds (*Calypte costae*) nest in Arizona; buff-bellied hummingbirds (*Amazilia yucatanensis*) nest in Texas.

Rufous hummingbirds (*Selasphorus rufus*) migrate through in spring and fall and many other, rarer species can be found in southeastern Arizona during nesting season, including the broad-billed hummingbird (*Cynanthus latirostris*), magnificent hummingbird (*Eugenes fulgens*) and violet-crowned hummingbird (*Amazilia violiceps*).

This region attracts the greatest variety of hummingbirds, with up to 15 species recorded at some time during the year, primarily in Arizona. The most widespread hummingbirds include the black-chinned, broad-tailed and

Because of its proximity to Mexico and the Central American tropics, the Desert Southwest attracts the greatest variety of hummingbirds, such as this broad-billed male.

Opposite: The Costa's hummingbird nests in the desert Southwest. This male is taking a rest from his courting duties.

Costa's from our "Big 8" list.

Why are there so many different kinds of hummingbirds in the Southwestern states? The answer has to do with the terrain and proximity to hummingbird wintering grounds. For birds

Making an Impression

Most birds use distinctive songs to carve out their territories. Because hummingbirds aren't songsters, male birds use another method to intimidate rivals and impress females, called the dive display. Each species flies its own distinctive pattern in the air, but the message is the same: Other males should stay away and females should settle in. Here are their various styles:

- Allen's male: begins with pendulum flights, then rises up to 100 ft. and descends in a J-pattern

- Anna's male: hovers, then flies up to 130 ft., followed by a fast oval-shaped plunge, ending with a squeak

- Black-chinned male: broad U-shaped arcs at about 25 ft., accompanied by shrill squeaks and droning of wings

- Broad-tailed male: power dives from up to 75 ft., accompanied by wing trill

- Calliope male: U- or J-shaped dive from up to 90 ft., loud whistle at bottom of dive

- Costa's male: a series of vertical, descending loops accompanied by a whistle sound, loudest at bottom of loop

- Ruby-throated male: repeated arcs from up to 40 ft. in air, with loud wing and tail sounds

- Rufous male: oval flight, repeated several times, accompanied by a rattling call and a popping sound made by tail feathers

migrating up through Mexico, this region is only a short flight away. And the mountains themselves attract the birds. Many species of hummingbirds spend the winter in mountainous terrain in the tropics and seek similar topography when looking for nesting sites. In addition, mountains offer a diversity of habitats as birds proceed to higher elevations or even to a different side of the mountain. The "sky islands" of Arizona—those tall, scattered peaks in the desert—host an abundance of hummingbird species.

Gardening challenges: With the great diversity in habitats and elevations in this region, it's not easy to generalize about gardening. The challenges include the low humidity and scarcity of rainfall, the hot, dry winds and summer's soaring temperatures. Native plants are the key to establishing a garden that looks lush and food-filled to hummingbirds, one that provides places to hide, perch and nest.

Because water scarcity is a major issue everywhere in this region, the wise gardener will seek out plants with low water needs. Other strategies for conserving this valuable resource include plant zoning—grouping plants with similar water needs together—and mulching to reduce evaporation. Using a drip system to irrigate the garden, as opposed to a sprinkler, also helps conserve water and reduce the amount lost to runoff. A water-conserving garden can display a broad range of blooming plants but we need to be careful to select non-thirsty plants and monitor our water use.

Good plant choices include the salvias

(*Salvia* spp.), aloe vera (*Aloe barbadensis*), which conveniently blooms in winter and spring, desert honey-suckle (*Anisacanthus thurberi*), Parry's pen-stemon (*P. parryi*), flame acanthus (*Anisacanthus wrightii*), chuparosa (*Justicia californica*) and ocotillo (*Fouquieria splendens*). Some of these, includ-ing the chuparosa and the penstemon, require desert-like conditions and will not thrive if your region has too much humidity and rainfall.

Salvia and penstemon are tough and, with just a little care, do well in Southwest gardens. Hummingbirds love the blooms of both these perennials.

A Hummingbird Garden for the Desert Southwest

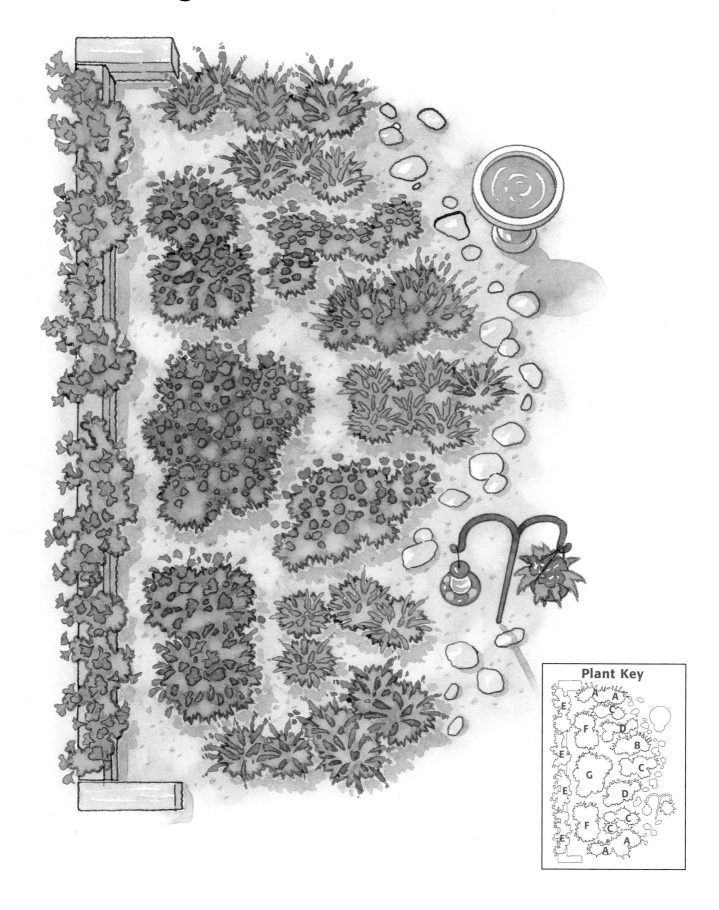

Plant Key

FLOWERS

Penstemons: **(A)** Rocky Mountain Penstemon (*P. strictus*), blooms May through July; Firecracker Penstemon (*P. eatonii*), blooms spring and early summer; Parry's Penstemon (*P. parryi*), spring bloomer; and many other penstemons

Hummingbird's mint (B) (*Agastache cana*), blooms summer to frost

Salvias: **(C)** Autumn Sage (*Salvia greggii*), blooms spring through fall; Little-leafed Sage (*S. microphylla*), blooms nearly year-round

California fuchsia (*Zauschneria californica*), blooms summer and fall

Indian paintbrush (D) (*Castilleja* spp.), blooms in summer

VINES

Trumpet Honeysuckle (E) (*Lonicera sempervirens*), blooms June to September or later

Red Morning Glory (*Ipomoea coccinea*), blooms summer and fall

SHRUBS

Desert Honeysuckle (F) (*Anisacanthus thurberi*), blooms spring through fall, sometimes winter in warmer areas

Ocotillo (*Fouquieria splendens*), blooms in spring

Chuparosa (G) (*Justicia californica*), blooms in spring

Introduce petunias in containers.

To bump your garden up to another level of brightness, add containers of showy annuals, such as petunias (*Petunia* spp.), snapdragons (*Antirrhinum majus*), begonias (*Begonia semperflorens*) and impatiens (*Impatiens* spp.).

There are many other good plants to consider for gardens in these regions. After your basic planting plan is established, you may wish to choose from the list at right to add variety to your garden, always keeping blooming times in mind as you proceed. Something in bloom in every season is the mantra of the successful hummingbird gardener.

Some Other Plants to Consider

Bouvardia (*Bouvardia ternifolia*)

Flowering Quince (*Chaenomeles speciosa*)

Texas Sage (*Salvia coccinea*)

Autumn Sage (*S. greggii*)

Lemmon's Sage (*S. lemmonii*)

Scarlet Sage (*S. splendens*)

Mexican Bush Sage (*S. leucantha*)

Crimson Columbine (*Aquilegia formosa*)

Pineleaf Penstemon (*P. pinifolius*)

Red-Hot Poker (*Kniphofia* spp.)

Turk's Cap (*Malvaviscus arboreus* 'drummondii')

Red Justicia (*Justicia candicans*)

Tree Tobacco (*Nicotiana glauca*)

Giant Hummingbird's Mint (*Agastache barberi*)

Coral Bean (*Erythrina herbacea*)

Desert Willow (*Chilopsis linearis*)

Mexican Honeysuckle (*Justicia spicigera*)

Shrimp Plant (*Justicia brandegeeana*)

Citrus Trees (*Citrus* spp.)

Red Yucca (*Hesperaloe parviflora*)

Foxglove (*Digitalis* spp.)

Some Notes on Hummingbird Behavior in These Regions

The Allen's hummingbird hugs the Pacific coastline as far north as southern Oregon (where there's some overlap with the rufous' nesting range). The Allen's has the most constricted range of any North American nesting hummingbird. They're early birds, beginning to arrive in January and continuing into April. They start heading southward fairly early, as well, beginning in July, with most concluding migration by September. An important food plant for the Allen's is the monkeyflower (*Mimulus* ssp.), a Pacific Coast native, as well as fuchsia-flowered gooseberry (*Ribes speciosum*) and twinberry honeysuckle (*Lonicera involucrata*). Males are known to be aggressive and quarrelsome; females build nests in oak and cypress trees and occasionally in vines.

The Anna's is one of the few nonmigratory hummingbirds on the continent. They're tolerant of human activity and are found year-round in their range, often in urban areas. Their range resembles a boomerang along the Pacific Coast as far north as Vancouver Island, British Columbia, and as far eastward as southern Arizona. These hardy birds begin nesting in winter and often have time to raise two or even three broods. Afterward, they move eastward for a time, to feast on mountain wildflowers in Arizona. Some even wander as far east as the Gulf Coast states. Important food plants include red-flowering currant (*Ribes sanguineum*), fuchsias (*Fuchsia* spp.) and tree tobacco (*Nicotiana glauca*). Insects make up a large proportion of the Anna's diet. Females build nests on tree branches and in shrubs and vines.

Black-Chinned hummingbirds have the broadest range of all the Western hummingbirds, occupying a broad swath from central Texas all the way to southern British Columbia. They're known as the birds of lower elevations early in the season, moving higher as flowers come into bloom. If competition is stiff from other hummingbirds, black-chins don't defend a feeding territory, instead traveling from food source to food source. Black-chins flock to ocotillo (*Fouquieria splendens*), desert honeysuckle (*Anisacanthus thurberi*) and tree tobacco (*Nicotiana glauca*). The birds arrive in late

Opposite: A male black-chinned hummingbird approaches the blooming branch of an ocotillo shrub.

March and April and have finished nesting by late summer. Females prefer to nest in oak trees or shrubs.

Costa's hummingbirds nest in desert habitats in southern California, Nevada and Arizona. These gorgeous little birds begin nesting in February and March and, because they're used to arid terrain, they aren't as dependent on proximity to water sources as are other hummingbird species. Some Costa's spend the winters in southern California and southwestern Arizona. Ocotillo (*Fouquieria splendens*) is an important food plant for the Costa's, as are desert willow (*Chilopsis linearis*) and chuparosa (*Justicia californica*). Females build nests in trees, shrubs, yuccas and cactus, raising one brood a year.

Calliopes, true birds of the mountains, appear as wildflowers come into bloom from early March to May. These high-elevation birds often nest near the timberline and are not frequent backyard visitors. Females build nests in evergreens, often anchoring them to pinecones. Nesting season can begin in late April and is completed by mid-August, after which the birds depart for Mexico. Calliopes, although fairly belligerent themselves, share much of their range with the aggressive rufous hummingbird. They often visit low-growing plants for nectar, probably as a way to avoid battles with the rufous. Calliopes can often be found feeding at penstemons (*Penstemon* spp.) and paintbrushes (*Castilleja* spp).

Rufous, the most northerly of our nesting hummingbirds is also the most belligerent, battling aggressively with broad-tailed, black-chinned and Costa's hummingbirds as the rufous migrates through the other birds' nesting ranges from February to May. They also duel with members of their own species in confrontations over feeding territories. Some rufous hummingbirds travel nearly 3,000 miles to nest as far north as Alaska and the Yukon. They're known to advance northward in short hops, proceeding as spring flowers come into bloom. Look for them to begin arriving in Washington in early March and in Alaska by early May. They feast on flowering currant (*Ribes* spp.), columbine (*Aquilegia* spp.) and salmonberry (*Rubus spectabilis*). After nesting, rufous hummingbirds tend to wander, with a number returning to the Gulf Coast and other southern states in fall and winter each year.

The broad-tailed is a fairly large hummingbird and an habitué of mountainous regions, arriving in Arizona and New Mexico in late February or early March, then slowly proceeding up mountainsides. Broad-tails often are found near scarlet sage (*Salvia splendens*), bouvardia (*Bouvardia* spp.), ocotillo (*Fouquieria splendens*) and columbine (*Aquilegia* spp.). These are familiar birds to mountain hikers, who see broad-tails foraging in alpine meadows. Nests are built on a low branch in either evergreen or deciduous trees.

Look for **buff-bellied hummingbirds** in the spring and summer in Texas's Lower Rio Grande Valley and the southeastern part of the state. The female builds her nest in a shrub or small tree such as live oak (*Quercus* spp.). In fall and winter, some buff-bellied hummingbirds move northward and eastward along the Gulf

Coast. They can be found feeding at Turk's cap (*Malvaviscus arboreus*), coral bean (*Erythrina herbacea*) and Texas sage (*Salvia coccinea*).

Unusual for North American hummingbirds, the males and females of this handsome species are similar in appearance.

A female broad-tailed hummingbird sips nectar from an Indian paintbrush flower in a mountain meadow.

6

Hummingbird Gardening: Great Plains and Mountain West

U.S.D.A. Hardiness Zones 3 to 8

Great Plains

Mountain West

**Broad-Tailed Hummingbird Female
At Honeysuckle**

A successful hummingbird garden offers nectar-producing flowers in all of the seasons that hummingbirds are in the area. In these two regions, where migratory hummingbirds can be found from spring through fall, this means having flowers available from frost to frost. And not just any flowers fill the bill—we need to have eye-catching, nectar-rich blooms for our tiny guests.

Gardening challenges: Gardeners and hummingbirds can confront some big challenges in the Great Plains and Mountain West. With four distinct seasons, the climate can be extreme, with wide temperature fluctuations between long, cold winters and hot, dry summers. Winter can be a dry period in some areas, but heavy winter snows will blanket the landscape in the north and at high elevations. The growing season is fairly short, bracketed by late spring freezes and early fall frosts, and rainfall is limited. In the Southern Plains areas, heat tolerance needs to be factored in when choosing plants, while in the north and at high elevations, plants will need to be frost-tolerant, with an emphasis on cool-season plants or plants that can be treated as annuals.

Soils tend to be either rocky or thick with clay, but the greatest challenge of all, in terms of gardening, is the scarcity of water that typifies this region. We need tough and resilient plants

for the Great Plains and Mountain West, and that frequently means natives—they've learned to survive short growing seasons, drought-like condi-

When creating a Western hummingbird garden, remember the type of natural habitat you're trying to replicate: lush alpine meadows with a wide variety of colorful blooms.

mingbirds visit in the wild, so they quickly recognize them as food sources in your garden. (It's as if they're thinking, "Hmmmm … there're some of those great penstemons and salvias, and while I'm down there, maybe I'll try some of that stuff with the little sign that says 'petunia.'")

Gardeners in the Great Plains region will need to be content with hosting hummingbirds as they rush through during spring and fall migration, since very few of the little birds stop to nest in this region. However, in the Mountain West, it's a different story, with four

tions and temperature extremes. Not only will plants native to your region require little supplemental water or food, but they're the plants hum- species regularly nesting here. The four are the black-chinned (*Archilochus alexandri*), broad-tailed (*Selasphorus platycercus*), calliope (*Stellula*

The country is big here, but you can still draw hummingbirds close.

calliope) and rufous (*Selasphorus rufus*) hummingbirds. This hummingbird abundance can probably be attributed to the mountains themselves, which offer a wide range of habitats and conditions for hummingbirds.

While the Southwest region has the highest number of species of hummingbirds, the Mountain West holds boasting rights for sheer numbers of the little birds. From Idaho's slopes to mountain meadows in the Canadian Rockies, the hills are alive with hummingbirds from spring to fall. There are reports from throughout the region of throngs of hummingbirds stopping at feeders on the way to their nesting grounds. Some gardens and feeders briefly host black-chinned, calliope and rufous hummingbirds in great numbers in spring.

Open for Business

Whether they find them in a garden or growing on mountain slopes, these migrants are drawn to penstemons (*Penstemon* spp.), columbines (*Aquilegia* spp.), salvias (*Salvia* spp.) and bee balm (*Monarda* spp.). Since many hummingbirds arrive before most gardens are in bloom, it's important to set out bright containers of annuals and/or hanging baskets with red and orange flowers early. This sends the message that your garden is open for the important business of providing food for the little birds as they rush to replace fat lost on migration and undertake the rigors of courtship and nesting.

Opposite: A female broad-tailed hummingbird feeds at a salvia flower. Salvias bloom early and long, making them important hummingbird plants both in the mountains and on the plains.

How Fast?

Hummingbirds fly in and out of view so quickly that we think of them as speed demons. However, some of this speed is illusory: Small objects seem to move faster than large ones traveling at the same speed. Wind-tunnel experiments have clocked hummingbirds at between 25 and 30 m.p.h., although they can achieve speeds of 60 m.p.h. in plunging dives. Compare this to the average speeds of other birds: ducks and geese, 50 m.p.h., and chickadees, 15 m.p.h.

Equally important is to have your hummingbird feeders filled and ready for the very first birds—try to hang feeders about two weeks before you saw the first hummingbird last year. Placing hummingbird feeders near flowers doubles your chances for drawing hummingbirds to your homemade nectar. Early spring and late fall are the times when hummingbirds could most use an energy boost. After a particularly cold spring night or a sudden frost, the calories in your nectar feeders just might make the difference between life and death for tiny birds that live so close to the edge.

Early Arrival

The hummingbirds arrive early, in April and May, and quickly establish feeding and nesting territories, with females raising the young birds without any help from males. By late August, as wildflowers fade from the Rockies, hummingbirds begin to head southward. With early scouts in spring and late stragglers in fall, the bird season is longer than the flower season, so we need to plan carefully to have something in bloom at all times between April and October.

Hang your nectar feeders by early April (and bring them indoors at night if temperatures are still dropping below freezing). But first, catch those hummingbird eyes with something dramatic, preferably a hanging basket of flowers. Many hummingbird gardeners report success with a pot or hanging basket of fuchsia (*Fuchsia* spp.), and hybrids such as 'Gartenmeister Bonstedt' make an excellent choice.

Our strategy early in the season is to draw the birds in with a splash of color, sustain them with our nectar feeders, then offer plants whose blooms provide nectar and attract small insects as the season progresses. We'll use natives wherever possible and supplement with blooms that attract hummingbirds without harm to the local ecosystem.

Also please note: In order to be the most hospitable hosts, we need to provide those other vital elements of hummingbird habitat as well.

Does your birdbath have a fountain or mister attachment for these air-borne bathers? Are there perching spots available nearby in shrubs and trees? Is there cover, in the form of thick shrub-bery and evergreens?

We've got some real climatic ranges in these two regions, and in the more southern and west-ern areas, just about anything grows. Heading north into the mountains, however, we're limited to plants that survive in Zone 3. A good average might be Zones 4 and 5, so let's use these two hardiness zones as our baseline.

Penstemon doesn't have to be red to attract hummingbirds. This purple 'Prairie Dusk' variety will do the job, too.

A Hummingbird Garden for the Great Plains and Mountain West

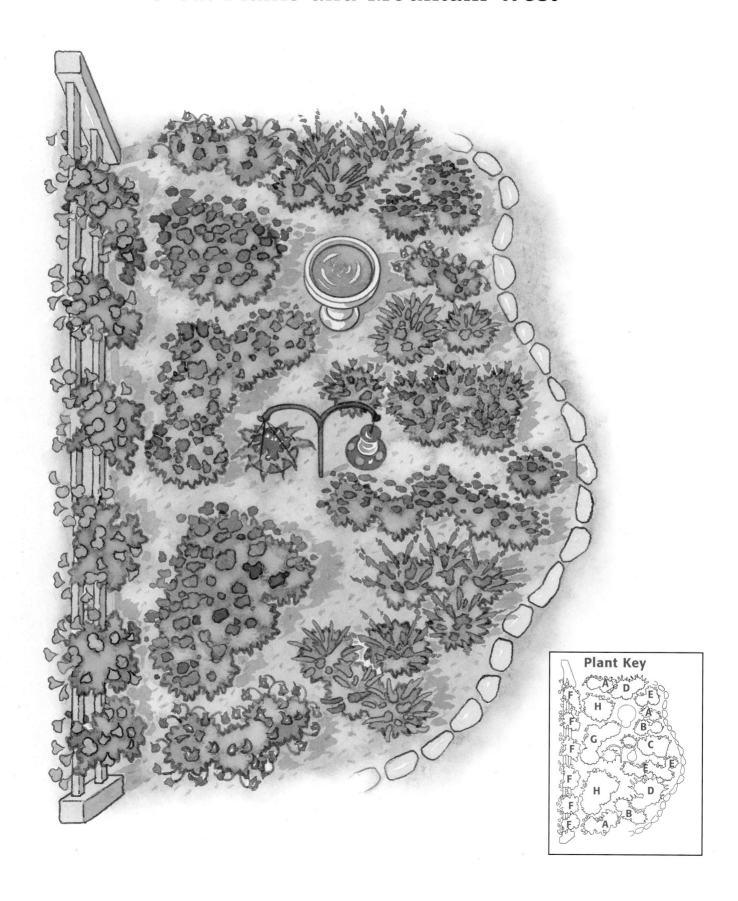

Plant Key

FLOWERS

Columbines: (A) Crimson Columbine (*Aquilegia formosa*), blooms spring and summer; Rocky Mountain Columbine (*A. caerula*), blooms spring and summer; Yellow Columbine (*A. chrysantha*), blooms spring and summer

Salvias: (B) Scarlet Sage (*Salvia splendens*), blooms summer until frost, often grown as an annual; Texas Sage (*S. coccinea*), blooms spring to frost

Scarlet Gilia (C) (*Ipomopsis aggregata*), blooms in summer

Penstemons: (D) Rocky Mountain Penstemon (*P. strictus*), spring and summer; Firecracker Penstemon (*P. eatonii*), spring and early summer; Pineleaf Penstemon (*P. pinifolius*), summer

Bee Balm (E) (*Monarda* spp.), summer

VINES

Tatarian Honeysuckle (*Lonicera tataria*) spring and summer

Morning Glory (F) (*Ipomoea* spp.), summer and fall

Bee balm (*Monarda*).

SHRUBS

Gooseberries and Currants (G) (*Ribes* spp.), bloom spring and summer

Honeysuckles (H) (*Lonicera* spp.), including Wild Honeysuckle (*L. ciliosa*), spring through fall

Fill in your starter garden with showy annuals, such as petunias (*Petunia* spp.), impatiens (*Impatiens* spp.) and zinnias (*Zinnia* spp.), and don't forget the power of containers of bright and showy annuals in early spring and late fall.

There are many other good plants to consider for gardens in these regions. After your basic garden is established, you may wish to choose one or several species from the list at right to add to your garden, always keeping blooming times in mind as you proceed. Something in bloom in every season is the mantra of a successful hummingbird gardener.

Some Other Plants to Consider

Coral Bells (*Heuchera* spp.)

Bleeding Heart (*Dicentra* spp.)

Scarlet Betony (*Stachys coccinea*)

Wild Bee Balm (*Monarda fistulosa*)

Cardinal Penstemon (*P. cardinalis*)

Beardlip Penstemon (*P. barbatus*)

Blue-Mist Penstemon (*P. virens*)

Pineapple Sage (*Salvia elegans*)

Desert Four-o'Clock (*Mirabilis multiflora*)

Purple Coneflower (*Echinacea* spp.), for the insects they attract

Hummingbird's Mint (*Agastache cana*)

Red Yucca (*Hesperaloe parviflora*)

Indian Paintbrush (*Castilleja* spp.)

Scarlet Monkeyflower (*Mimulus cardinalis*)

Blazing Star (*Liatris* spp.)

Snowberry Bush (*Symphoricarpos albus*)

California Fuchsia (*Zauschneria* spp., especially 'Orange Carpet')

Cardinal Flower (*Lobelia cardinalis*)

Willow Herb (*Epilobium angustifolium*)

Red-Hot Poker (*Kniphofia* spp.)

Spider Flower (*Cleome* spp.)

Some Notes on Hummingbird Behavior in These Regions

Black-chinned, broad-tailed, calliope and rufous hummingbirds can be found in the western mountains and western edges of the Great Plains during breeding season. Broad-tailed hummingbirds establish nesting territories in the mountains, while some rufous hummingbirds nest in western Montana and northern Idaho (although most head to time-honored sites in the Pacific Northwest). The calliope migrates through the Great Plains region on its way to nesting sites in western Montana and central and northern Idaho. And the black-chinned has an extensive breeding range across the West, where it is the most common hummingbird.

Black-Chinned: These birds primarily nest in western Colorado, Utah, Nevada and Idaho. Where their range overlaps those of other species, the black-chins tend to be the underdog. If competition is stiff, black-chins give up on defending a territory, instead traveling from food source to food source, a strategy called trap-lining. Black-chins flock to ocotillo

A male black-chinned hummingbird visits a nectar feeder. Black-chins are probably the least aggressive of the mountains and plains hummingbirds. That means you should place multiple feeders, in different areas of the the garden, so that black-chins have a place to go.

A female broad-tailed hummingbird visits a honeysuckle flower. Broad-tails are true mountaineers, preferring the high country over any other kind of habitat.

(*Fouquieria splendens*), desert honeysuckle (*Anisacanthus thurberi*) and tree tobacco (*Nicotiana glauca*) along their migratory routes. Black-chins begin arriving in western states in early May, quickly reaching the northern limit of their range by mid-May and finish nesting by summertime. Females prefer oaks for their nests.

Broad-Tailed: This is the largest of the "Big 8" hummingbird species and is the common nesting hummingbird of the Rockies. They begin arriving in Colorado and Nevada in late April and in Idaho, the northern limit of their range, by late May. They often are found near flowering shrubs such as honeysuckle, as well as scarlet sage, bouvardia (*Bouvardia ternifolia*), ocotillo and columbines. Mountain hikers frequently encounter this species foraging in alpine meadows. Nests are built on a low tree branch in either evergreen or deciduous trees. They leave when the mountain wildflowers are gone and are seldom found in the region later than September.

Opposite: A male calliope hummingbird hovers near a nectar feeding station. To identify a calliope, look for the distinctive streaked throat.

Calliope: A bird of the northwestern mountains as far north as British Columbia, the calliope appears as wildflowers start to bloom, arriving in Idaho and Montana in mid- to late May. These are birds of the high elevations, often nesting near the timberline, and are not frequent backyard visitors. Females build nests in pines, firs, spruces or hemlocks and often anchor them to pinecones. Nesting season can begin in late April and is completed by mid-August, after which the birds begin departing for Mexico. Calliopes, although fairly belligerent themselves, share much of their range with aggressive rufous hummingbirds. They often visit low-growing plants for nectar, probably as a way to cope with the pugnacious rufous. Calliopes can often be seen feeding at penstemons, butterfly bush (*Buddleia* spp.) and snowberry bush.

Rufous: These are intolerant little birds, battling aggressively with any and all species of hummingbirds as they migrate through their nesting territories. They also duel with members of their own species in confrontations over feeding territories. They have to be tough to withstand the rigors of their long-distance migration, flying as far as Alaska and the Yukon to nest. They move across much of western North America and begin arriving in Montana and Idaho near the end of April. They often feast on flowering currant (*Ribes* spp.) and columbine. Fall migration starts early, with many rufous hummingbirds heading southward in late July and August. Rufous hummingbirds tend to wander after nesting season, with a number showing up in Gulf Coast and Southeastern states in winter year after year.

Give 'em Shelter

As more becomes known about hummingbirds, greater attention is being given to that key word, shelter (or cover). When we think of hummingbirds, we think of their boundless energy and tireless zipping and hovering around nectar sources. But that incredible level of activity takes a toll, which is why hummingbirds spend up to 80 percent of each day resting on perches.

So shelter or cover is very important to them. Wild birds favor wild places, so those of us in urban settings have to work a bit harder on this point. A backyard featuring a carpet of mowed grass, several clumps of flowering plants and a hanging nectar feeder just doesn't have much appeal for hummingbirds. They prefer the layered look, with a plethora of shrubs and vines, some tall trees, especially evergreens, a few leafless branches for perching, plants that provide soft material for nest making and a riot of flower color to ensure a good nectar supply. A birdbath with a mister or fountain works like a charm, and having plenty of spiders busily spinning webs and stringing silk lines is another plus.

7

Hummingbird Gardening: Continental East and Southern Canada

U.S.D.A. Hardiness Zones 2 to 7

Ruby-Throated Hummingbird, Male
At Pine Tree

Only one species of hummingbird—the ruby-throat—is common in this huge region. Here, a male feeds at a trumpet creeper flower.

One species of hummingbird inhabits this ecoregion, knitting together a range from Nova Scotia to North Carolina, Missouri to Minnesota and even extending as far to the northwest as southern Alberta, Canada. This vast area is the home of the ruby-throated hummingbird (*Archilochus colubris*), making identification an easy matter from spring to fall. You don't need a field guide to identify hummingbirds in this region, you only need a map: If you see a hummingbird during nesting season, it's a ruby-throat.

The entire eastern half of the United States is the exclusive nesting grounds of the ruby-throat. Some western Canada gardeners at the very edge of the ruby-throats' range may also host rufous (*Selasphorus rufus*) and calliope hummingbirds (*Stellula calliope*) during migration periods. These vivid little birds are regularly found in 38 states and seven Canadian provinces.

As they move northward in spring, ruby-throats often arrive before any flowers are in bloom. These savvy birds have learned another way to sustain themselves until there are flowers to provide nectar. They drink from the small wells chiseled into tree trunks by the yellow-bellied sapsucker (*Sphyrapicus varius*). The sap that flows into the wells is a sweet syrup very similar to flower nectar.

Sapsucker Connection

In fact, researchers who study birds are noticing that hummingbirds have a close relationship with sapsuckers. There simply wouldn't be hummingbirds in the northern portions of this region without sapsuckers, since they drill the holes that fill with the sap that sustains the little birds until flowers come into bloom. It's been said that without sapsucker wells, ruby-throats wouldn't be found farther north than Missouri. (In the West, the black-chinned hummingbird is similarly reliant on native sapsuckers for early-spring survival.)

The ruby-throat is one of the most fearless of hummingbirds in an already fearless family, often lapping up nectar from flowers even as a gardener works nearby. There are many reports of ruby-throats landing on hats, shoulders and even fingers in their relentless quest for food. Like all hummingbirds, they exhibit strong fidelity to a feeding or nesting territory. So if someone in Boston, Mass., or Bemidji, Minn., for example, tells you that "her" hummingbird

returned to the garden this spring, she could very well be right: The same hummingbirds return year after year to the same backyards, often on the very same date. There are always new birds on the lookout for food sources and nesting sites in the migrant stream as well. These

Early in spring, when hummingbirds have returned but the flowers aren't blooming much, sap dripping out of sapsucker holes provides important nourishment for hungry hummers.

are the hummingbirds born the previous summer, now eager to establish their own feeding and nesting territories.

There are hummingbirds that travel farther on migration, especially that long-distance champion, the rufous hummingbird, but none of the other North American species accomplishes anything like the ruby-throat: flying nonstop across the Gulf of Mexico. Most ruby-throats accomplish this astonishing feat of athleticism twice each year, covering a distance of at least 500 miles each time (depending on the route taken).

Because ruby-throats heading northward in spring often outrun the blooming season, it's important to hang baskets and set out containers of flowers early and have feeders ready and waiting. Hanging baskets featuring bright fuchsias (*Fuchsia* spp.) and impatiens (*Impatiens* spp.) will provide instant color and an open invitation to any hummingbirds passing through the area.

Anticipate the Demand

A general rule of thumb is to put out nectar feeders about two weeks before the usual arrival date for ruby-throats in your area, since some birds are always retro-punctual. If you live in Tennessee, this means putting feeders out mid-March for an April 1 arrival date. In Pennsylvania, hang feeders the first week of April for birds due April 21, in central

A male ruby-throated hummingbird approaches a feeder hung near a basket of impatiens.

Saved by Sapsuckers

In the northern parts of some hummingbird ranges, the birds arrive in spring several weeks before flower nectar is available. Hummingbirds are smart, and they've figured out a way to get the sugar they need for quick energy (plus the insects they need for protein). They follow sapsuckers around, the yellow-bellied (*Sphyrapicus varius*) in the East and the red-naped (*S. nuchalis*) and Williamson's (*S. thyroideus*) in the West. Sapsuckers drill shallow holes, also called wells, around tree trunks, then tree sap flows freely into the wells. Hummingbirds survive in early spring by shadowing sapsuckers to find their wells. They then drink the tree's "nectar," which has nearly the same sugar concentration as most flower nectar. The sap attracts tiny insects, as well, so hummingbirds visiting sap wells can fill up on both their food groups.

It's been said that without sapsucker wells to tide ruby-throated hummingbirds over for several weeks until flowers come into bloom, the northernmost limit of this bird's range would be in Missouri instead of southern Canada.

Wisconsin, set feeders out mid-April for May 1 birds and in the Maritimes, late April is a good time for feeder placement. If nighttime temperatures are still dropping below freezing, you can bring baskets and feeders in at dusk, then return them in the morning, just after dawn.

On the Lush Side

Once hummingbirds have discovered your garden, you can bribe them to stick around by providing a succession of blooming plants throughout the summer and fall. If you've visited a hummingbird garden at a local park or arboretum, you'll have noticed how generous the plantings are. Instead of a few, widely spaced blooms, they emphasize a lush profusion of blossoming annuals, perennials, vines, shrubs and even trees. Although most backyard gardeners don't have the space or the budget to duplicate these public gardens, we can learn from their example. Group plants together and try for the most lush-looking landscape you can achieve. This reassures the little birds that they're not going to run out of nectar during their visit.

Annuals, perennials, vines, shrubs and trees create the mosaic of color and vegetation needed to attract hummingbirds.

If you want hummingbirds to nest in your yard or garden, you need to plant enough security cover and offer enough water to make females (this one is probing flower tubes) feel safe.

If you're lucky enough to have a hummingbird nesting in your yard or in the neighborhood, you'll be able to enjoy visits all summer long. However, if you live in an urban area or far from a water source, chances for enticing a female to nest in your garden are slim, since nesting ruby-throats prefer seclusion, usually in wooded areas near water. No matter what, watch for migratory birds in April and May, then again August through September. In autumn, you may notice many birds that lack the characteristic brilliant red throat patch typical of males of this species. Many of these will be the young birds born just months earlier.

Gardening challenges: These vary by latitude, but generally this four-season region enjoys a middle range of most natural elements. Rainfall is usually adequate, except in drought years. The growing season shortens as hummingbirds travel north, of course, but there is no shortage of blooming plants to choose from. Summers can be hot and winter temperatures and length range from moderate to very cold and long, but native plants can easily survive these extremes. Soils range from rich to depleted, but good gardening practices, especially composting and mulching, will enhance any garden in the region.

One note of caution: Although this certainly isn't an arid region, some areas can experience droughts of several years' duration. Just as for the rest of the continent, however, water scarcity is a looming problem, even in Minnesota, which boasts of its "10,000 lakes." Our rapidly growing human population is drawing down aquifers and other natural water sources at an alarming rate. Savvy gardeners will lean toward plants that require little supplemental water to help

Opposite: Monarda (also known as bee balm) attracts hummingbirds with its bright red color and profusion of nectar-rich, long-lasting blooms.

ensure that there's enough water for gardens—and hummingbirds—in the future.

Generally, that means an emphasis on native plants, those that have adapted over eons to the conditions in our own backyards. It would be great if we all could plant the colorful penstemons native to the West, since they're so popular with hummingbirds and so drought-tolerant. But most penstemons would wilt under the greater rainfall and humidity in many parts of this region. Similarly, the jewelweed that hummingbirds flock to in late summer and fall

prefers streamsides and other moist environments, making it an iffy choice for most backyard gardens.

The Continental East and Southern Canada encompass some real climatic ranges, and in the more southern and western areas of this region, just about anything grows. Heading north into the mountains, however, we're limited to plants that survive in Zone 3. A good average might be Zones 4 and 5, so we'll use these two hardiness zones as our baseline.

A Hummingbird Garden for the Continental East and Southern Canada

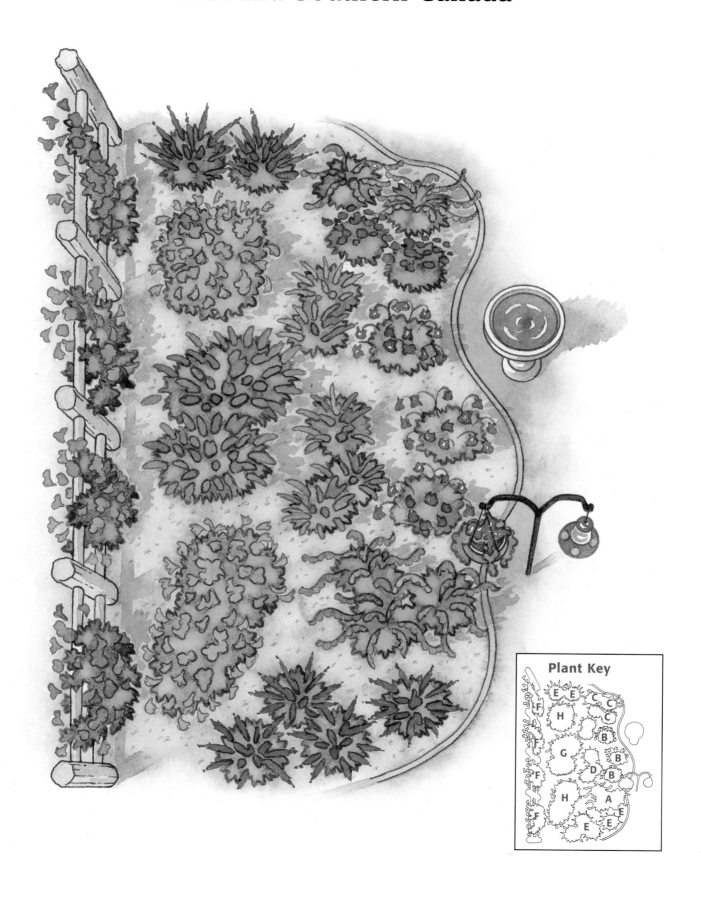

Plant Key

FLOWERS

Bleeding Heart (A) (*Dicentra* spp.), early spring

Columbines: (B) Wild Columbine (*Aquilegia canadensis*), Yellow Columbine (*A. chrysantha*), spring and summer

Bee Balm (C) (*Monarda* ssp.), summer to fall

Scarlet Sage (D) (*Salvia splendens*), summer to fall

Cardinal Flower (E) (*Lobelia cardinalis*), Blue Cardinal Flower (*L. siphilitica*), summer to fall

VINES

Trumpet Creeper (F) (*Campsis radicans*), June to fall

Morning Glory (*Ipomoea* spp.), summer and fall

SHRUBS

Lilac (*Syringa* spp.), spring

Japanese Flowering Quince (*Chaenomeles japonica*), spring

Trumpet creeper (*Campsis radicans*).

Butterfly Bush (G) (*Buddleia alternifolia*), summer to fall

Trumpet Honeysuckle (H) (*Lonicera sempervirens*), spring through fall

A hanging basket full of bright impatiens, fuchsia or other blooms will be a key factor in putting your garden on the hummingbird map, especially in northern areas, where little is in bloom as ruby-throats arrive on migration. Fill in your starter garden with showy annuals, such as petunias (*Petunia* spp.), impatiens and zinnias (*Zinnia* spp.).

There are many other good plants to consider for gardens in this region. After your basic garden is established, you may wish to choose one or several species from the list at right to add to your garden, always keeping blooming times in mind as you proceed. Something in bloom in every season is the mantra of a successful hummingbird gardener.

Some Other Plants to Consider

Coral Bells (*Heuchera* spp.)

Blazing Star (*Liatris* spp.)

Dropmore Honeysuckle (*Lonicera* x *brownii*)

Spotted Jewelweed (*Impatiens capensis*), not usually found in gardens, but if growing nearby, preserve it

Hardy Fuchsia (*Fuchsia magellanica*), in containers

White Fireweed (*Epilobium angustifolium*)

Crested Beard-Tongue (*Penstemon eriantherus*)

Flowering Crabapple (*Malus* spp.)

Hostas (*Hosta* spp.)

Amethyst Violet (*Browallia speciosa*)

Impatiens (*Impatiens* spp.)

Foxglove (*Digitalis* spp.)

Azaleas (*Rhododendron* spp.)

Snowberry (*Symphoricarpos albus*)

Red Buckeye (*Aesculus pavia*)

Autumn Sage (*Salvia greggii*)

Other Salvias (*Salvia* spp.)

Phlox (*Phlox* spp.)

Hollyhock (*Alcea rosea*)

Coneflower (*Echinacea* spp.), for insects

Weigela (*Weigela* spp.)

Some Notes on Hummingbird Behavior in This Region

Ruby-Throated Hummingbird: Ruby-throats begin arriving along the Gulf Coast in early March, progressing northward in a wave along latitudinal lines until reaching the northern limits of their range in Canada in mid-May. Females often build nests in wooded areas near water, in either a pine or deciduous tree, but also in more open areas, even in parks. Curious and unafraid, they are easily enticed by nectar feeders. They favor salvias (*Salvia* spp.), cardinal flower, trumpet creeper, bee balm, columbines (*Aquilegia* spp.) and spotted jewelweed, among others. With such a vast breeding range, these birds find food in many habitats.

Ruby-throated hummingbirds can't resist the blooms of the cardinal flower (*Lobelia cardinalis*) whenever it is offered.

Hummingbirds 101

Don't be daunted by lists of plants, blooming dates or anything else that makes attracting hummingbirds seem complicated. Hummingbirds are so easy to please that we can offer good hospitality without much effort or expense.

Basically, you want to plant flowers that produce plentiful nectar, hang sugar water feeders to supplement the blooms and choose trees, shrubs and vines to provide cover and attract insects. The final item on this short list is water, especially flowing or dripping water.

There's only one no-no: pesticides. Don't use them anywhere in your yard or garden, ever. Pesticides kill all insects, the good, the bad and the beautiful (such as butterflies). Hummingbirds can pick up the residue as they feed and become ill or even die.

Anyone can garden for hummingbirds. Some flowers, a little water, a few vines and shrubs, a place to hang a nectar feeder or two, all arranged in a relaxed way that's pleasing to you … that's all a hummingbird needs.

Hummingbird Gardening: Humid South and Tropics/Subtropics

U.S.D.A. Hardiness Zones 7 to 11

8

Ruby-Throated Hummingbird, Immature Male
At Firebush Plant

It might seem that a region with such a benign climate and lush planting possibilities would be able to boast a wide variety of hummingbird species. But this region, like the Continental East to the north, is limited by its geography. Migratory hummingbirds travel a direct route into the southern United States to head for their spring and summer nesting grounds. But as they depart Central American countries in the early spring, if they head eastward, the Gulf of Mexico lies directly in their path. This 500 miles of open water is a physical barrier of immense proportions for such tiny birds. Most species of migratory hummingbirds proceed to the north along a west-

They Fly Alone

Hummingbirds do not migrate in family groups. Instead, males depart first, followed some weeks later by females and finally juvenile birds set off on their migratory journeys. Parent birds do not guide their offspring on their first long flights, as do other species such as sandhill cranes (*Grus canadensis*). Incredibly, young hummingbirds find their way alone to traditional wintering areas in the tropics, an indication of the power of instinct. Although large numbers of hummingbirds may drop down to feed in an area during migration and many may depart at the same time, hummingbirds are solitary migrants, each conducting its own journey.

erly axis and end up raising their young far to the west of the Mississippi River.

Only one hummingbird veers eastward out of Mexico during spring migration, and that's the ruby-throat (*Archilochus colubris*), the only species to nest east of the Mississippi River.

To reach the southern United States, ruby-throats accomplish something awe-inspiring: flying nonstop across 500 miles of water. This seems like a nearly impossible feat for a tiny bird that weighs barely one-tenth of an ounce. Ruby-throats gorge themselves before taking off across the Gulf, putting on a fat layer to fuel the long flight. At takeoff, they may weigh half

Opposite: Hummingbird numbers in this region can explode overnight, as hungry migrants arrive from their dash over the Gulf of Mexico. Have your feeders ready!

again their normal weight. The fat burns up during the 18 to 20 hours of nonstop flight required to navigate the Gulf. A strong headwind can make the difference between arriving safely on land or plummeting exhausted into the sea.

Millions of ruby-throats flood into the Southeast each spring on their dash toward feeding and nesting territories. Many stop in Gulf Coast states to raise their families, while many others head farther north, populating the entire eastern half of the United States and southern Canada.

One note: Although ruby-throats may cross into the southern tip of Florida, this region's one patch of tropical or subtropical climate, the birds don't stay to nest. So in discussing nesting birds in this chapter, we'll be focusing on the Humid South region.

Easy to Please

Ruby-throats are resilient, adaptable birds that have learned to make the best of what they find wherever they land. They're flexible in their tastes and exploit a variety of nectar-producing plants. Having only a single species of hummingbird makes it easy on gardeners in this region: Plant what ruby-throats prefer and you can pretty much sit back and watch them commandeer your garden. This is true whether you live near

Vegetation is lush and thick in this region. To work essential flowers into the mix, try creating colorful perennial borders that back up to thick cover.

Raleigh, North Carolina; Jacksonville, Florida; Shreveport; Louisiana; or Montgomery, Alabama.

They flock to red buckeye shrubs (*Aesculus pavia*) in the spring, cypress vine (*Ipomoea quamoclit*) in the summer, flowering maple (*Abutilon pictum*) in the spring and fall and cardinal flower (*Lobelia cardinalis*), bee balm (*Monarda* spp.) and trumpet creeper (*Campsis radicans*) all summer long.

The Arkansas Ozarks are particularly rife with ruby-throats both in migration and during nesting season. This region hosts so many hummingbirds during fall migration, their population augmented by the juvenile birds hatched just weeks earlier, that many gardeners set out extra feeders to accommodate them. In areas with heavy activity, some gardeners report that the little birds drain four to six feeders each day, more than double the usual rate.

Gardening challenges: Gardeners in the Humid South enjoy a warm climate and a lengthy growing season, but they also face a number of challenges. There's a broad array of planting conditions, with soils that range from

Flowers with a tropical origin, such as the shrimp plant (*Justicia brandegeeana*), grow well in this warm and humid region, and pull in the hummingbirds.

called xeriscaping, which relies on native plants, shrubs and trees to reduce water usage.

Sharing Their Domain

There's been a major change in hummingbird behavior in this region that indicates that the Humid South is no longer the exclusive domain of the ruby-throated hummingbird, at least after nesting season. Bird banders are providing evidence that there's a little-understood winter hummingbird phenomenon going on in this region. Many species of Western hummingbirds from the "Big 8" list (and other species as well) are turning up in Gulf Coast states beginning in November each year. And these aren't merely

sandy on the coast to loamy wetland conditions inland and everything in between. The flat coastal plains contrast with heavily forested areas and the highlands and valleys typical of the Ozarks and the Great Smoky Mountains.

Back-to-back drought years have compelled many gardeners to become creative about their use of water, with some even capturing and holding it in more sophisticated versions of the old rain barrel. Summer's high heat and humidity dictate the choice of plants that don't wilt easily under such conditions. And there's increased interest in the water-saving landscaping approach

An immature male ruby-throat sips nectar from firebush flowers (*Hamelia patens*) in Mississippi.

Keep Feeders Hanging

Many gardeners in the Humid South live along major hummingbird migratory flyways. This means they see masses of ruby-throated hummingbirds in the spring and fall. Some people worry that feeders left out late in the fall will cause some hummingbirds to stay around and miss migration, later succumbing to winter's cold. Nothing could be further from the truth. Feeders don't stop hummingbirds from migrating—the birds leave when their hormones tell them it's time. Leaving feeders out for several weeks after the main migration is a help to stragglers that may lack the fat reserves needed to continue on migration. Your feeders could give these birds a much-appreciated energy boost. Instead of harming hummingbirds, feeders left out in autumn may save some hummingbird lives.

confused birds or birds blown off course, because banded birds have been recorded returning to the same gardens winter after winter.

It will be fascinating to learn more about this behavior as time goes on: What routes do the hummingbirds use from the West to the Southeast? Do they fly down to wintering grounds in Mexico, then head northeastward if food is scarce? No one has the answers at this point, but gardeners and bird banders in Gulf Coast states and farther inland are on the case.

Summer and Winter Gardens

This change in hummingbird behavior is leading to some changes in how gardeners behave as well. In the Gulf states and other parts of the South, an increasing number of gardeners are cultivating two gardens. There's one for the spring, summer and fall visits by ruby-throats, then another garden with frost-tolerant plants for winter hummingbird visitors.

In the Southeast, the rufous (*Selasphorus rufus*) and black-chinned hummingbirds (*Archilochus alexandri*) are the most frequent winter strays, but buff-bellied hummingbirds (*Amazilia yucatanensis*) also appear regularly. Gardeners also sometimes see Allen's (*Selasphorus sasin*), Anna's (*Calypte anna*), calliope (*Stellula calliope*), broad-tailed (*Selasphorus platycercus*), blue-throated (*Lampornis clemenciae*), broad-billed (*Cynanthus latirostris*) and magnificent hummingbirds (*Eugenes fulgens*), as well as the occasional wintering ruby-throat.

Cover Is Key

These birds are looking for backyard gardens that feature cold-hardy blooms, nectar feeders and plenty of cover. In fall and winter, thick evergreen cover is much more important than in the other seasons, as the little birds seek shelter on cold nights and during cold rains and ice storms.

This region has only a small patch of subtropical climate, in southern Florida, and hummingbirds seem to find the area somewhat inhospitable. Ruby-throats avoid southern

Florida in nesting season, and the only other hummingbirds found there are very occasional strays from the Caribbean.

During fall migration, gardeners in the Gulf states can find themselves inundated with hungry ruby-throats looking for a quick burst of energy from feeders and flowers before attempting the Gulf of Mexico. Hummingbirds can be found

Canna (*Canna* 'Striata'), cardinal flower (*Lobelia cardinalis*) and black-eyed Susans (*Rudbeckia fulgida*) combine to make a beautiful summer garden for southern hummingbirds.

en masse at many of the salvias (*Salvia* spp.), shrimp plant (*Justicia brandegeeana*) and standing cypress (*Ipomopsis rubra*). In warmer areas, gardeners attract fall and winter birds with flowering maple, Mexican cigar plant (*Cuphea micropetala*), several kinds of late-blooming honeysuckle (*Lonicera* spp.) and giant Turk's cap (*Malvaviscus penduliflorus*). Gardeners farther north can grow many of these plants in containers and bring them indoors when nighttime temperatures plunge.

An extremely popular plant with fall migrants is spotted jewelweed (*Impatiens capensis*), and many ruby-throats even seem to time their fall migration to coincide with this plant's blooming period. Many gardeners report that if a stand of jewelweed is nearby, hummingbirds ignore their feeders and blooms. Jewelweed thrives in damp, shady environments, and gardeners who can offer these conditions will find the plant grows easily.

Ruby-throats are very curious and not at all fussy birds. A garden plot is not required to bring them in—an apartment balcony with hanging baskets and container plants, as well as a feeder or two, will do the job just as well.

A Hummingbird Garden for the Humid South—Spring to Fall

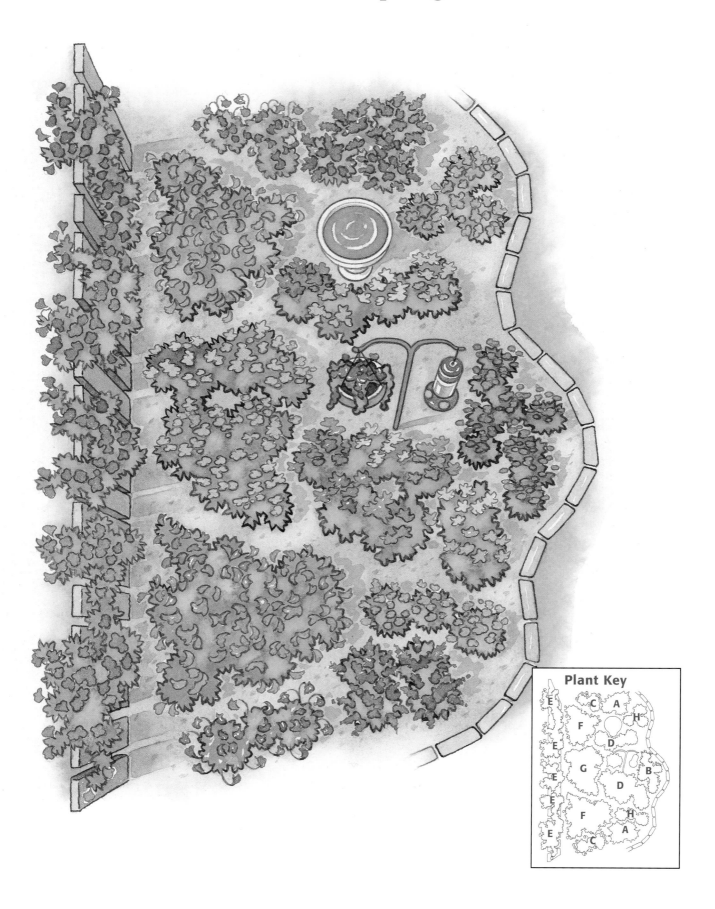

Plant Key

FLOWERS

Cardinal Flower (*Lobelia cardinalis*), summer to fall

Salvias: (A) Scarlet Sage (*Salvia splendens*), Texas Sage (*S. coccinea*), Pineapple Sage (*S. elegans*), Anise Sage (*S. guaranitica*), summer to fall

Bee Balm (B) (*Monarda* spp.), summer to fall

Wild Columbine (C) (*Aquilegia canadensis*), spring and summer

Scarlet Hibiscus (D) *Hibiscus coccineus*), mid-summer to frost

VINES

Trumpet Creeper (E) (*Campsis radicans*), June to fall

Red Morning Glory (*Ipomoea coccinea*), summer and fall

Foxglove (*Digitalis* spp.).

SHRUBS

Mexican Cigar Flower (*Cuphea* x 'David Verity'), summer to frost

Honeysuckle Fuchsia (F) (*Fuchsia triphylla*), constantly

Flowering Maple (G) (*Abutilon pictum*), year-round, heaviest in fall and spring

Azaleas (H) (*Rhododendron* spp.), spring and summer

Annuals can be used to fill in your garden with splashes of bright color. Try impatiens (*Impatiens* spp.), annual phlox (*Phlox drummondii*), zinnias (*Zinnia* spp.) and spider flower (*Cleome* spp.).

In order to make sure that we're offering our best hospitality, we need to provide those other important elements of hummingbird habitat, as well. Does your birdbath have a fountain or misting attachment for these airborne bathers? Are there perching spots nearby in shrubs and trees? Is there cover in the form of thick shrubbery and evergreens? Only when we can answer 'yes' to each of these questions can we be assured that we've created hummingbird habitat.

There are many other good plants to consider for gardens in this

---

Some Other Plants to Consider

Mexican Bush Sage (*Salvia leucantha*)

Coral Bean (*Erythrina herbacea*)

Pentas (*Pentas* spp.)

Flame Azalea (*Rhododendron carolinianum*)

Foxglove (*Digitalis* spp.)

Lemon Bottlebrush (*Callistemon citrinus*)

Witch Hazel (*Hamamelis* spp.)

Shrub Verbena (*Lantana* spp.)

Mimosa (*Albizia julibrissin*)

Pink Root (*Spigelia marilandica*)

Crabapple (*Malus* spp.)

Campion (*Silene* spp.)

Red Buckeye (*Aesculus pavia*)

Shrimp Plant (*Justicia brandegeeana*)

Butterfly Bush (*Buddleia alternifolia*)

Buttonbush (*Cephalanthus occidentalis*)

Turk's Cap (*Malvaviscus arboreus* var. 'drummondii')

Standing Cypress (*Ipomopsis rubra*)

Spotted Jewelweed (*Impatiens capensis*)

Bromeliads (*Bromelia* spp.)

A Hummingbird Garden for the Humid South—Winter

Plant Key

region. After your basic garden is established, you may wish to choose one or several species from the list on page 147 to add to your garden, always keeping blooming times in mind as you proceed. Something in bloom in every season is the mantra of a successful hummingbird gardener.

Plants for Late Fall and Winter Gardens

Flowering Maple (A) (*Abutilon pictum*), nearly year-round

Shrimp Plant (B) (*Justicia brandegeeana*), blooms in winter (hard to find, ask for cuttings from someone's garden)

Mexican Cigar Plant (C) (*Cuphea micropetala*), fall and winter

Pineapple Sage (D) (*Salvia elegans*), fall and winter

Mexican Bush Sage (D) (*Salvia leucantha*), fall and winter

Winter Honeysuckle (E) (*Lonicera fragrantissima*), winter to spring

Mexican Cigar Flower (*Cuphea* x 'David Verity'), summer to frost

Some Notes on Hummingbird Behavior in This Region

Ruby-Throated Hummingbird: Ruby-throats by the hundreds may suddenly appear in spring and fall, stopping to build fat reserves as they follow traditional migratory paths through

Salvia leucantha.

the Southeastern United States. In spring, they begin arriving along the Gulf Coast in early March and spread northward in a steady wave. Southbound birds begin to appear in July and reach a peak in mid-August. Females often build nests in wooded areas near water, in either a pine or deciduous tree, but also in more open areas, even in parks. Curious and unafraid, they are easily enticed by nectar feeders. Ruby-throats tend to "stack up" along the Gulf Coast in autumn, feeding and fattening up for the flight across the Gulf. They fly nearly 2,000 miles to spend the winter in Mexico and Central America. Some ruby-throats spend the winter in Georgia, Louisiana and northern Florida.

9

Feeders, Feeding Strategies and Uninvited Guests

Smart gardening practices attract hummingbirds to your home and yard. Smart feeding practices help keep hummingbirds around ... and also pull them right where you can see and enjoy them most.

Broad-Tailed And Rufous Hummingbirds
Competing At Feeder

You won't be able to find the perfect hummingbird feeder on a shelf at your local bird feed retailer or garden supply store. That's because Mother Nature holds the exclusive patent: She alone produces the flowers that deliver nature-made nectar for a burst of energy for hummingbirds. Nature's delivery system is the best because flowers produce fresh nectar on a daily basis. Cleaning isn't an issue, because depleted flowers fade and fall, so there's no fermentation, bacteria or mold to worry about. And there's no waiting for hummingbirds to catch on that there's nectar inside, as there often is with artificial feeders, since hummingbirds instantly recognize flowers as a source of nectar.

However, nectar is nectar, whether provided by flowers or feeders, and feeders do have an important role to play in our gardens. They're invaluable early in the spring, when many hummingbirds are moving northward ahead of the blooming season. Feeders help birds survive during drought periods and cold snaps. They're useful during nesting season, when female hummingbirds need food for themselves and their twins and appreciate a reliable source nearby.

Feeders are a good way to diffuse the power of an aggressive hummingbird that commandeers a patch of flowers and drives off other hummingbirds. And nectar feeders in the fall help hummingbirds put on the fat needed for their long and arduous migrations.

Nectar feeders are a good way to supplement your garden's flowers, shrubs and trees. In fact, whatever your circumstance, whether it's a patio with several containers of blooms and some hanging baskets or a lavish flowering landscape, nectar feeders help increase your garden's "magnetism." Almost nothing could be easier than mixing up a batch of sugar water and pouring it into feeders for your whirring guests.

Keep It Clean

However, there is one hard-and-fast rule governing the feeding of artificial nectar to hummingbirds, and it's very important to the birds' health and willingness to make return visits. What's the most single most important aspect of hummingbird feeding? Is it choosing the appropriate feeder size and shape? Is it having the prettiest, most ornamental feeder on the

Opposite: If you clean them regularly and stock them with fresh nectar solution, your feeders will keep your hummingbird visitors both happy and healthy.

How Early to Feed?

It's nearly impossible to put out hummingbird feeders too early in the season. Experts recommend hanging them outdoors at least two weeks before hummingbirds are due in your area. Along the Gulf Coast, that could mean hanging feeders as early as mid-February for the first ruby-throated hummingbird (*Archilochus colubris*) migrants, while Tennessee residents should get their feeders out in mid-March.

Out West, gardeners in southern California may have feeders out year-round for the nonmigratory Anna's (*Calypte anna*), then hang additional feeders in mid-December for migrating Allen's hummingbirds (*Selasphorus sasin*) and other migrants such as calliopes (*Stellula calliope*) that may visit as they move through beginning in March.

If nights are still cold enough to freeze the sugar solution, bring feeders indoors overnight.

---

block? Or is it most important to mix the correct proportion of sugar to water? The answer is … none of the above. The most important element in feeding hummingbirds is cleanliness.

This point can't be emphasized too strongly—nothing is more important than keeping your hummingbird feeders clean and the sugar syrup fresh. If you're used to feeding songbirds, you may not be aware that nectar spoils much more quickly than birdseed does, and nectar feeders need regular, thorough cleaning. If you can't afford the time to clean your hummingbird feeders frequently, then do yourself and the birds a favor and get out of the hummingbird feeding business. Dirty feeders do more harm than good.

Pros and Cons

Your first consideration in selecting a feeder should not be how attractive it looks but how easy it is to clean. Ask for advice at the store where you purchase bird feeders. And don't buy a nectar feeder without first taking it apart yourself to determine how easy it will be to disassemble, clean and reassemble at home. If it's difficult or cumbersome to take apart, you'll find yourself avoiding this important task.

As more and more people become interested in feeding hummingbirds, an ever-increasing number of feeder designs are appearing on retailers' shelves and in catalogs. There are elegant hand-blown glass feeders that seem designed to appeal more to gardeners than hummingbirds. These are pretty, but they break easily and they're difficult to clean. There are large feeders that promise less maintenance, but these are appropriate only if you have heavy hummingbird traffic. Otherwise, the sugar syrup will begin to spoil before the birds have consumed it all.

Some feeders are ceramic, and their major drawback is that you can't easily determine when they need filling and/or cleaning. And there are feeders with all sorts of decorative touches and screens touted as bee guards—although these often turn out to be pretty effective at *attracting* insects.

Clean Is a Commitment

The people who have regular hummingbird visitors are the same people who commit to regular cleaning of their feeders. Please don't put out a feeder and let it hang all summer without any maintenance. If hummingbirds take a sip of spoiled sugar syrup, they're not likely to visit again. And there's the risk that molds or bacteria in an unclean feeder could sicken the little birds. So if you're going to feed hummingbirds, make the commitment to wash feeders regularly.

Whatever the activity level, feeders need to be cleaned and refilled at least every three days and usually much more frequently, especially in hot weather. During a hot week, every-other-day or even daily rinse-outs may be required. Unless you have a multitude of hummingbird visitors that drain your feeders daily, you're probably going to need to toss leftover sugar syrup and clean and refill the feeders before they've been emptied by birds. No matter how recently you replaced the sugar solution, if it begins to look cloudy, run right out and bring the feeder in for cleaning and replace the syrup.

Be diligent about cleaning your feeders' individual feeding ports. Small brushes are available just for the purpose.

How Clean?

How clean is clean? Take each feeder apart and rinse all parts in hot water on a regular basis. If any mold is visible, scrub it off or soak the feeder in a very mild vinegar or bleach solution (1 part vinegar or bleach to 9 parts water). Give the feeder a thorough rinsing and let it dry. (Some say not to use soap because hummingbirds can detect even the tiniest soap deposit; soap isn't needed, so it's probably best not to use it.) Many people have two sets of hummingbird feeders so one batch can be soaking or drying while the other is hanging outdoors. And remember: You can extend the "shelf life" of the sugar syrup by hanging feeders in the shade.

At least once a month, give each feeder a thorough cleaning, soaking it in a mild bleach solution for an hour or more, then rinsing well before refilling. Taking feeders apart, washing, rinsing and drying: that's what it's all about.

It's best to keep things simple and functional. Start with a small feeder and see how many birds visit. Once you have an idea about the level of hummingbird traffic, you may choose to set out a larger feeder or several feeders. Buy sturdy feeders that are easy to hang and have as few detachable parts as possible (these can get lost or broken during filling and cleaning).

The Magic Nectar Formula

What's the best hummingbird food? The easiest and least expensive food is one you can make right in your own kitchen. The nectar formula is a simple one: 1 part white table sugar to 4 parts water. That's all you need to remember: 1 to 4, sugar to water. Many of you have been using this formula for years, boiling sugar and water together for a couple minutes, then refrigerating the syrup before filling feeders. Many dedicated feeders of hummingbirds now feel that it's better to boil the water, turn off the heat, then stir in the sugar, to avoid evaporation that could concentrate the mixture.

One final note on sugar syrup: In reading a gardening book recently, I came across the

All you need to make hummingbird nectar is sugar, water and a container to mix it in. Nectar solutions are also available, but plain sugar works just as well. The choice is yours!

astonishing claim that homemade sugar syrup is "junk food," possibly even harmful to hummingbirds. If you encounter a statement like this one, please don't believe it. That writer is seriously misinformed. The sugar syrup we make is nearly indistinguishable from the nectar produced by flowers, both in terms of chemical makeup and nutrients. Hummingbirds need nectar for quick energy. Their other dietary needs—proteins, vitamins and minerals—are supplied by the insects they eat. You don't need to spend money on mixtures that purport to provide a balanced diet, because hummingbirds are perfectly capable of achieving that themselves.

To help attract insects to your garden, you might try setting out pieces of banana and melon, either in a hanging mesh bag or on a plate. And remember, don't undo all the work you've done to attract hummingbirds and insects by using pesticides on your yard or garden. If you kill off all the insects, hummingbirds won't find your garden attractive and the poisons in the pesticides can harm the little birds as well.

Honey Is a No-No

Some people who've been feeding hummingbirds for years swear that the birds can detect and will reject syrup made with beet sugar, so to be on the safe side, use only cane

> ## Taking a Census
>
> During the busy migration seasons, hummingbird feeders may attract clouds of little birds battling for a high-energy drink. Is there any way to estimate how many hummingbirds are visiting your feeders each day? We can't simply count the number of birds appearing over a given period of time, since hummingbirds make many repeat visits to replenish their energy supplies, averaging about four feeding trips per hour. A straight count would mean counting the same birds several times. But there is a way to calculate the total number of birds, devised by people who've been banding and color-marking hummingbirds for years: Count the number of birds you see at any one time, and multiply by six. This should give you an approximate number of the different birds drinking your sugar syrup in a day.

sugar. There's no need to invest in commercial mixes since plain old cane sugar and water is what hummingbirds prefer.

Please don't use anything other than table sugar—no sugar substitutes, no honey and no red dyes. Some people figure that if sugar is good, then honey is better, being a more "natural" product. But honey is very bad for hummingbirds. It spoils quickly when mixed with water, and the molds this produces can lead to illness or even death for hummingbirds. Another minus: Honey will attract bees from near and far. So don't use honey. It's just as well to avoid red coloring, too. We don't yet know if dyes are completely harmless and they're simply not needed.

Bees and wasps are unwanted guests. Drinking nectar solution isn't the problem; scaring hummingbirds away is. Wipe up spills on your feeders, and replace any feeders that leak nectar solution.

Bees, Wasps and Ants

Unfortunately, hummingbirds aren't the only creatures in nature that like a sweet drink. Bees, wasps and ants are always looking for nectar, too. Even though bees prefer a much sweeter solution (their favorite flowers tend to have nectar that's twice as sweet as those that hummingbirds prefer), bees and wasps are drawn to nectar feeders. Aggressive wasps can keep hummingbirds at bay and bees mobbing the feeder ports will discourage even the toughest hummingbird.

To discourage insects, be vigilant about wiping up any spills that accumulate on the feeder. If a port or seam leaks, it's time to toss the feeder because such leaks draw insects. It's also important to pry off or paint over any yellow elements on your feeders because yellow is an insect magnet. (Better yet, don't buy a feeder with yellow elements.) Try hanging a separate feeder nearby, one with plenty of yellow pieces, and fill it with a sweeter syrup (maybe 2 parts water to 1 part sugar) for bees and wasps. Chances are they'll flock to this feeder and leave the hummingbird feeders alone.

Avoiding Ants

To deter ants, place an ant moat on the hanging wire above the feeder to prevent them from proceeding to the nectar. Fill the moat with water, and small birds like chickadees will visit for a drink, an added benefit. Avoid smearing petroleum jelly or other sticky substances on the hanging wire, the moat or the feeder itself. Sticky stuff can get on hummingbirds' wings and impair their ability to fly. A hummingbird that can't fly will be unable to feed, possibly leading to its death. If the feeder is anchored to a pole, place an upside-down ant moat low on the pole and smear the inside with petroleum jelly. Since it's upside down, it won't bother the birds. (Some feeders now even incorporate an ant moat into the design.)

Where fire ants are a problem underneath feeders, take steps to eliminate spillage. This might mean substituting a saucer-style feeder for the hanging-bottle variety, since bottles allow the sugar syrup to expand on hot days and drip steadily to the ground, drawing in the ants.

To keep ants away, hang your hummingbird feeder and place an ant moat (shown here) above it. Ants don't fly or swim, so they can't get onto the feeder.

More Insect Tips

In some parts of the country, bees and wasps hanging around hummingbird feeders are a real headache. Other tips for keeping them at bay include hanging nectar feeders in the shade because bees prefer to feed in sunlight (and the syrup will last longer if it's not in the sun). Some

Is Yellow Mellow?

Two colors come into play when considering hummingbird food and feeders. Red is one color factor: Should you buy red-dyed prepared nectar mixes that promise added proteins and minerals? These mixes aren't necessary, because a hummingbird's menu of nectar and insects provides a well-rounded diet. And red dyes aren't known to be harmful, but neither are they known to be safe, so let's avoid them. It's so easy and so much cheaper to make your own sugar syrup, anyway.

As for the color yellow, some hummingbird feeders feature "bee guards," usually screens made of yellow plastic. Unfortunately, these work more like "bee attractors," since yellow is a color bees see easily and associate with food. Either remove any yellow parts on a hummingbird feeder or purchase feeders without any yellow.

people put out a shallow bowl of highly concentrated sugar solution to attract and drown bees and wasps. Be aware that bee guards are more trouble than they're worth and may actually attract bees. Some hummingbirds are put off by the guards and won't visit feeders that have them. One other negative: The plastic screens could potentially damage hummingbirds' beaks.

What works the best at keeping out insects? A red, saucer-type feeder seems to be the most effective at barring bees and wasps. The saucer bowl is deep enough to prevent insects from reaching the sugar syrup, but hummingbirds can easily do so with their long tongues.

Squirrels are cute, but hummingbird feeders weren't designed to accommodate the ingenious and acrobatic little rodents. To start, don't place a hummingbird feeder this close to a tree.

Other Freeloaders

Other kinds of birds can be nuisances at hummingbird feeders, especially orioles, finches and woodpeckers. Some folks don't mind feeding nectar to these birds, but if you do, hang feeders that lack perches. An even more effective strategy is to mount a perch-less feeder on a pole. Because other birds are unable to hover, this will reserve the feeder for hummingbirds and should prevent the larger birds from draining the feeder.

Squirrels are always on the lookout for a free meal, and these opportunistic rodents love a sip of nectar. Some possibilities for foiling squirrels include hanging feeders from tree branches high enough so the critters can't leap onto them. Use a long hanging wire with a squirrel baffle attached so that they can't shinny down. If feeders are mounted on a pole, add a squirrel baffle underneath the feeder.

If you find your feeders empty every morning, you may be feeding bats overnight. If this

Opposite: Orioles are beautiful, and not quite so problematic as squirrels. But the mere presence of orioles scares hummingbirds away from feeders. Options include using hummingbird feeders that don't have perching spots, offering orioles their own jelly feeders, or putting out orange halves for them.

Why Migrate at All?

In northern climates, it's pretty easy to see why hummingbirds head south in the autumn: The insects they need for protein disappear and flowers with nectar die back as the temperature falls. But in warmer areas, where flowers bloom nearly all year and insects are plentiful, why don't hummingbirds just stay put?

The answer has to do with the way the little birds evolved. They're birds of the tropics that have gradually expanded their range into the temperate zone for the rich food sources and unoccupied nesting niches available farther north. The spring and summer explosion of insects in northern climates fuels the quick growth and development of nestlings, and the profusion of blossoms makes nectar readily available. As both insects and nectar begin to wane, hummingbirds already are putting on fat stores for the long journey southward.

---

bothers you, you could bring the feeders inside each evening and hang them out again before dawn. Or you could resign yourself to supplementing the diet of these important pollinators.

A Final Tip or Two

What's the best material to use for hanging feeders? Experts recommend noncorrosive metal or plastic-coated wire. Other kinds of materials degrade quickly in weather and sun. If you live in a windy area, hanging feeders will sway in the breeze, spilling some nectar with each swing. Pole-mounting the feeder will prevent this problem.

Another feeder tip: The sugar syrup will last longer if you don't hang feeders in direct sunlight. But keep in mind that hummingbirds are used to feeding at flowers in the sun, so avoid dense shade for hanging feeders. It's best to choose a location that is in the sun early in the morning, then in the shade as the day advances and the temperature rises.

The Best Feeder?

Now that we know some of the challenges, what's the best feeder to select for hummingbirds? You'll notice that there are plenty of different styles and sizes on the market. One basic rule is to start small. Choose a feeder that holds from 6 to 12 ounces of nectar. This should be enough for several days, unless you live along a major migratory route and have hundreds of visitors.

Perches? Some feeders have perches, others lack them. Since hummingbirds have the ability to hover, perches aren't really necessary. However, being able to perch to feed saves a bird energy. This can be important on cold days and first thing in the morning when energy stores are low after a long night. (But then again, perches also can be used by larger birds, such as orioles, and they can quickly drain a feeder.)

Glass or plastic? Consider how easy the feeder is to clean and how likely you might be to break the glass. Remember, hummingbirds aren't looking for aesthetics, they're only interested in a quick drink for energy.

Bottle or saucer type? Again, ease of cleaning is the major consideration, and saucer feeders are generally much easier to clean. Secondly, saucers are less likely to leak or spill nectar—and spills attract unwanted guests. The upside-down bottle type of feeder is based on creating a vacuum; the sugar syrup inside can expand on hot days, leading to leaks. Saucer-type feeders offer a pool of nectar that hummingbirds dip down into to drink. This type of feeder doesn't drip and therefore won't attract insects as easily.

Feeders come in all shapes and sizes. Try different models to see which work best for your hummingbirds! Shown here: bottle style, both big (1) and small (6); saucer (2); bottle style with "flower" feeding ports (3); and decorative but functional feeders (4 and 5).

Pretty or functional? Go with the functional feeder, since hummingbirds aren't concerned with how pretty a feeder might be, and make sure you can easily see the nectar inside. If you can't see the nectar, you won't be able to tell if the syrup is spoiling or when the feeder is empty.

My preferred feeder is a small, red plastic saucer type, with no yellow parts. It's easy to clean, the nectar level is easy to see, it has no perches and seems to suit the hummingbirds just fine.

Avoiding Battles

If you host a large number of hummingbirds and territorial battles frequently break out, having more than one feeder can bring greater harmony to the backyard. Place the feeders in different locations around the yard, putting them behind sight barriers so one bold bird can't try to dominate them all. For example, position one feeder near a flowering bush, another on the other side of the house and a third behind a sight barrier, maybe a vine-covered arch. You

might also try placing several feeders at different heights, one at 3 ft. or less, another about 6 ft. high and a third hanging 12 to 15 ft. off the ground. This works particularly well if you have several different species visiting your feeders.

Another strategy that seems to work when multiple birds are around is to bunch three or more feeders close together. The little birds quickly learn that it's impossible to defend all the feeders from all other hummingbirds, so they meekly feed together.

Adding 'Magnetism'

If you put out a feeder and hummingbirds avoid it, the problem may be that they simply don't recognize it as a food source. It's best to hang or mount feeders near cover and near flowering plants and perching sites. This increases the chances that hummingbirds will find your feeders and learn that they contain a sweet reward. Keep in mind that individual hummingbirds show various degrees of willingness to visit nectar feeders. Some never visit feeders, while others take to them right away.

Opposite: Hummingbirds can get downright ornery and competitive. Here, a male broad-tail attacks a rufous hummingbird for feeding rights. Use multiple feeders, at different heights and in different locations, if you have many hummers around.

Hummingbird Tongues

Hummingbird tongues are forked, grooved and long. Like woodpecker tongues, a hummingbird's tongue is so long that it winds around inside the back of its head when not in use. When bird banders have a hummingbird in hand, they can brush aside head feathers, showing through the bird's translucent skin how the tongue runs in a loop over the top of the bird's skull. This never fails to astound bystanders.

Contrary to popular belief, hummingbirds don't suck up nectar. Instead, they lap it up, at a rate of about 13 licks per second. Because hummingbirds don't have much space for storing food, they consume many small meals a day instead of a few large ones. They eat, then rest, then eat some more, repeating this process more than 60 times a day.

Having a source of water nearby, especially dripping, misting or falling water, is a real drawing card for hummingbirds. If they stop in to bathe, they may give your feeders a try. We should also remember that hummingbirds need places to perch and to hide. This means a bare branch or two not far from feeders and birdbath, and dense shrubbery and/or trees surrounding your property.

And one last point, maybe the most important of all, in terms of your payback for being a good host to hummingbirds: Hang feeders where you can watch and enjoy them from inside the house. If you have a breakfast nook that looks over a deck, hang a flowering basket and nectar feeder so you can see them. Ditto if you spend a great deal of time in a home office—hang a feeder or two within view.

10
Hummingbird Gardens Aren't Just for Hummingbirds

When you garden for hummingbirds, you also create habitat for other wildlife.

Scarlet Tanager

A garden that is good for hummingbirds is good for other wildlife, including butterflies and songbirds.

Now it's time to sit back and relax in the habitat you've created. You've planted hummingbird-attracting flowers and added some shrubs and vines for cover. Backing up your garden are evergreen shrubs and trees to provide much-needed nesting sites and additional shelter. There's a mist attachment or fountain in the birdbath splashing hummingbirds as they fly through the spray.

You've kept in mind birds' preference for the layered look in landscaping, with tall trees for their initial "drop down," mid-level plants for perching and resting and flowering plants closer to the ground for feeding. If you aren't rewarded with visits from your region's hummingbirds right away, it should be only a matter of time.

By creating a haven for hummingbirds, you've done another very important thing, especially if most of the plants in your garden are native to your region: You've created habitat. As more and more of us choose native plants in place of horticultural exotics, we're quite literally improving the environment. Indigenous vegetation supports a whole web of wild creatures, each of which is reliant on the others for survival.

There's a whole lot more going on in our gardens than is usually visible. At ground level, there are bacteria and microbes that keep the soil healthy. This, in turn, allows all kinds of insects and other living things, such as worms, to thrive. Many insects in our gardens are beneficial, performing natural functions of keeping garden pests under control (think of the relationship between ants and aphids) and serving as food items themselves for larger creatures (such as hummingbirds).

Gardening Like Mother Nature

Keeping things natural benefits us all: birds, pets, people and the world at large. Garden plants need healthy soil and native insects to help them fight pests and disease. If we pull out a can of weed-killer or pesticide every time we notice an insect infestation or a weed in the lawn, we create dangerous conditions that cascade down through this chain of life. Chemicals kill not only the insects we regard as pests but also beneficial insects such as lady beetles and lacewings. And pesticides kill butterflies, a beautiful complement to any garden. Herbicides and pesticides may persist in the environment for some time after a single application, and they can be taken up by the plants that hummingbirds rely on for nectar.

You've heard the word biodiversity and this is what it's all about—letting natural things thrive

Few Chemicals Are Safe

We'll be doing all of nature a favor if we spurn chemicals for the yard or garden. Avoid chemical use yourself and ask your lawn-care company for a list of what chemicals they use on your property. If they can't tell you, switch to a service that can. Many people assume that if a chemical is for sale at the local nursery or hardware store, or is being applied by a lawn maintenance company, it's been certified as safe. Nothing could be further from the truth. The federal government grants licenses for new chemicals but does not certify the safety of such products. Weed- and insect-killers are assumed to be innocuous until overwhelming evidence to the contrary proves otherwise.

Once chemicals run off our yards and gardens into storm sewers, they enter rivers and lakes and harm all sorts of other creatures—including ourselves. The deadly effect is the same whether you apply the chemicals yourself or hire a lawn service to do it.

In the hummingbird/wildlife garden, the more natural you keep things, the better. Relax!

A monarch butterfly sips nectar from a purple coneflower. He's not really competing with his hummingbird neighbors.

and not doing unnatural things that interfere with nature. Many of us know these things; now here's our chance to help in our own backyards, by returning a small pocket of land back to nature.

Wafting Butterflies

Many of the same nectar-producing plants visited by hummingbirds also attract butterflies. And butterflies, in most regions, are creatures of

Opposite: Butterflies and hummingbirds both love flowers. This Eastern tiger swallowtail rests on a honeysuckle blossom.

summer. So even if hummingbirds only visit during spring and fall migration, there'll be butterflies wafting around your garden throughout the summer. Most of the flowers that attract hummingbirds also bring in nectar-loving butterflies. You may see painted ladies (*Vanessa cardui*), monarchs (*Danaus plexippus*), common buckeyes (*Junonia coenia*), swallowtails (*Papilionidae* spp.) and many others feeding at your honeysuckle (*Lonicera* spp.), purple coneflower (*Echinacea angustifolia*), milkweed (*Asclepias* spp.), bee balm (*Monarda* ssp.) and, of course, butterfly bush (*Buddleia* spp.).

If you notice some "hummingbirds with antennas," your garden has attracted some handsome sphinx moths. Often called "hummingbird moths," many of these flying insects are active in the daytime, unlike most other moths. They're about the same size as or a bit smaller than hummingbirds and they visit some of the same plants, but their flight is much less energetic and is nearly silent. One of the more familiar, the white-lined sphinx moth (*Celerio lineata*), found across most of the United States, lives up to its name: It has white stripes extending back over its head and stripes across the back. Since moths' wings beat at a much slower rate, they don't have the blurry effect of hummingbird wings. Although sphinx moths look a great deal like hummingbirds, the moth antennas are a dead giveaway—hummingbirds don't have them.

The Night Shift

Many other moths are in our gardens working the night shift. As darkness falls, there's an unseen changing of the guard. Butterflies settle into roosts in tall grasses or underneath broad leaves, and night moths emerge from leaf litter,

This hummingbird moth (more formally known as the sphinx moth) sips sugar water from a hummingbird feeder.

tree trunks or twigs where they've spent the day. They're out there under cover of darkness, feeding on the same nectar that hummingbirds covet, but we don't usually see them.

Here's a way to detect the moths visiting your garden at night: Cover a flashlight with yellow or red plastic film and stroll through the garden using the low illumination to pick up shining eyes. To increase your chances of seeing moths, put out a dish of rotting fruit (banana and peaches work well) and see how many moths show up for a lick. (This works in daylight with butterflies, too.)

Hummingbird gardens, by design, have a long and colorful blooming season. The flowers are attractive to butterflies and moths and other kinds of birds. (An aesthetically beautiful garden is one of the most peaceful, relaxing places for humans, too, especially important in stressful times.)

Songbirds such as this scarlet tanager find the trees, shrubs and laid-back feel of a good hummingbird garden to their liking.

Songbird Haven

With moving water in your birdbath or pond and the shelter provided by the vines, shrubs and trees in your yard, you have the perfect habitat for many songbirds as well. Baltimore orioles (*Icterus galbula*), Bullock's orioles (*Icterus bullockii*) and other species of orioles are fiends for nectar, possibly even becoming pests at your hummingbird feeders. They can easily be diverted by orange halves and grape jelly. Scarlet tanagers (*Piranga olivacea*), summer tanagers (*Piranga rubra*) or Western tanagers (*Piranga ludoviciana*) may

Water is essential to any hummingbird garden, and it benefits more than just the hummers. This flow works to attract a group of thirsty cedar waxwings.

stop in for a sip, and gray catbirds (*Dumetella carolinensis*) may be lurking in the undergrowth.

Catbirds, so secretive during nesting season, are easily drawn to a naturalized garden with plenty of shrub and vine cover. Some kinds of warblers (*Parulidae* spp.) and vireos (*Vireonidae* spp.) are attracted by a tangle of vines and a water source. Keep your eyes open for thrashers (*Mimidae* spp.) and other songbirds.

Birds are naturally curious and are always on the lookout for new sources of food and water. They need to drink frequently, and they need to bathe. That mister or fountain in your birdbath or pond will be almost irresistible to songbirds as well as to hummingbirds.

A Balanced Diet

Good habitat attracts another important element of a bird garden—insects. Tiny insects make up a goodly proportion of the hummingbird diet, so you don't want to do anything to discourage them. Insects will thrive in a pesticide-free garden with a variety of plants, especially native plants. You shouldn't have to worry about insects taking over—native plants have native controls. Some gardeners even go so far as to put out rotting fruit, such as melon and discarded banana skins, to attract fruit flies and other insects. Hummingbirds act like miniature flycatchers when they detect a cloud of gnats or fruit flies, snapping up the protein and vitamins that supplement their nectar diet.

The 'People Factor'

And now for one of the most important players in any hummingbird garden—you, the gardener. Make sure you can easily see your garden and the visitors it attracts. Position plants and nectar feeders so they're visible as you look out from the breakfast nook, living room or home office. Many people have a patio outside their kitchen or living room windows, and a patio can form the core of an attractive but compact garden. Hang a feeder or two near the windows, add a hanging basket or two and place containers of nectar-filled plants in the corners. You might even be relaxing on your patio as hummingbirds zip in to dine.

If more space is available, you can plant hummingbird garden beds that can be viewed from indoors, backing them up with shrubs and some evergreens. You want your garden to be a sanctuary both

Don't forget about people. Place plants, feeders and water at locations that make it easy for you and your guests to enjoy your wild visitors. These hummers are broad-tails.

An abundance of blooms is what you're looking for ... and what the hummingbirds want.

for you and for birds and other creatures.

Hummingbird gardens appeal to hummingbirds and humans. We all seem to respond to an abundance of red, orange and pink blossoms, as well as the vibrant blues and purples that also attract the little birds. Many hummingbird flowers are beautiful in their own right—we'd plant them even if they didn't have such a following in the hummingbird world. After all, a major reason for planting a flower garden is for the aesthetic pleasure it brings us and our friends and neighbors, and hummingbird gardens can be awesomely gorgeous.

Going 'Wild'

Try to put aside any Type A impulses in planning and maintaining your hummingbird garden. Get over the need to pull every weed, shear every shrub and line up flowers in neat rows. Let things go a little wild in the garden, an approach that more closely mimics Mother Nature's. Those shrubs really don't need much pruning, and let's see where that vine wants to go naturally. Plant flowers in clumps instead of

rows, and arrange them with shorter plants in front, taller plants in back. This is a more pleasing look for humans and appeals to hummingbirds' natural feeding patterns.

Go ahead and deadhead blossoms to encourage plants to bloom as long as possible. But at the end of the blooming season, leave plant spires and stems standing. They will not only be a source of winter interest but provide a wealth of winter food for seed-eating birds such as finches (*Fringillidae* spp.), chickadees (*Paridae* spp.) and others.

Cut the Grass

Whether urban, suburban or rural, there are other ways we can go gently in our own backyards. One is by reducing the amount of space taken up with nonnative turf grasses, with their heavy reliance on fertilizers and water. Many regions already are facing the issue of water scarcity, and it's coming soon to a neighborhood near you. The biggest environmental issue of this century is predicted to be a shortage of clean water.

This is another reason why native plants make such good sense: They've learned to thrive with the amount of rainfall that's natural to their region, requiring little or no supplemental watering. And they've adapted to the local soil conditions, meaning they shouldn't need much in the way of "store-bought" fertilizers.

Another way we can help the environment is by reducing our reliance on lawn maintenance equipment, such as lawn mowers and leaf blowers, many of which are major polluters. In fact, most lawn mowers are several times more polluting than an automobile. So the less we need to use these environmentally unfriendly machines—by reducing or eliminating the area given over to grass and making good use of fallen leaves as mulch and compost—the cleaner the air will be.

Use more native plants and less nonnative turf. Get away from using herbicides and pesticides. These are the keys to creating good, healthy hummingbird habitat. Shown: male rufous hummingbird.

Conclusion

A female ruby-throated hummingbird approaches a patch of bee balm.

The Only Real Rule: Have Fun

We hope you've had as much fun reading this book as we had researching, writing and editing it. Without a doubt, hummingbirds are some of the most engaging, fascinating and beautiful creatures in nature. It seems that everyone loves these fierce, fearless and intense little birds. They inspire us to connect with them by planting the flowers they prefer for nectar and hanging nectar feeders to add to our garden's attractiveness.

A male rufous hummingbird perches at a feeding station.

We've learned that hummingbirds regard our hanging or pole-mounted feeders as supplements to their everyday diet of flower nectar and insects. Thus, if we want to attract hummingbirds to our yards, we should, first and foremost, offer the plants they recognize as food sources. Catch their eyes and their interest and many of them will learn to visit our nectar feeders, too. Red is an important color for a hummingbird garden (and feeder) and moving water is a real magnet, as well.

Every garden in the country has at least one species of hummingbird flying over it at some time during the year, so the odds are good that hummingbirds will visit your yard and garden in the spring, summer or fall. Hummingbirds are, in fact, easier to attract than many songbirds.

We hope we've convinced you that it's not at all difficult to create hummingbird habitat and that doing so benefits you, hummingbirds, other birds and the entire natural world. Whatever the season and whatever your region, you can start now to plan a garden for some of the smallest and most wondrous creatures in nature.

Hummingbird gardening need not be complex. Just select some flowers and feeders, plant some shrubs, offer some water and you'll be in business. The hummers will come!

Hummingbird Journal

Year: _____

Date of First Hummingbird: _____

Spring Migration Notes: _____
_____

Other Significant Dates: _____
_____

Plants Hummingbirds Preferred: _____
_____
_____

Other Habitat Changes and Notes: _____
_____
_____

Hummingbird Behavior Observations:_____
_____
_____
_____

Fall Migration Notes: _____
_____

Date of Last Hummingbird:_____

Hummingbird Journal

Year: _____

Date of First Hummingbird: _____

Spring Migration Notes: _____

_____

Other Significant Dates: _____

_____

Plants Hummingbirds Preferred: _____

_____

_____

Other Habitat Changes and Notes: _____

_____

_____

Hummingbird Behavior Observations: _____

_____

_____

_____

Fall Migration Notes: _____

_____

Date of Last Hummingbird: _____

Hummingbird Journal

Year: _____

Date of First Hummingbird: _____

Spring Migration Notes: _____
_____

Other Significant Dates: _____
_____

Plants Hummingbirds Preferred: _____
_____
_____

Other Habitat Changes and Notes: _____
_____
_____

Hummingbird Behavior Observations: _____
_____
_____
_____

Fall Migration Notes: _____
_____

Date of Last Hummingbird: _____

Hummingbird Journal

Year: _____

Date of First Hummingbird: _____

Spring Migration Notes: _____
_____

Other Significant Dates: _____
_____

Plants Hummingbirds Preferred: _____
_____
_____

Other Habitat Changes and Notes: _____
_____
_____

Hummingbird Behavior Observations:_____
_____
_____
_____

Fall Migration Notes: _____
_____

Date of Last Hummingbird:_____

Hummingbird Journal

Year: _____

Date of First Hummingbird: _____

Spring Migration Notes: _____
_____

Other Significant Dates: _____
_____

Plants Hummingbirds Preferred: _____
_____
_____

Other Habitat Changes and Notes: _____
_____
_____

Hummingbird Behavior Observations: _____
_____
_____
_____

Fall Migration Notes: _____
_____

Date of Last Hummingbird: _____

Hummingbird Journal

Year:_____

Date of First Hummingbird: _____

Spring Migration Notes: _____
_____

Other Significant Dates: _____
_____

Plants Hummingbirds Preferred:_____
_____
_____

Other Habitat Changes and Notes: _____
_____
_____

Hummingbird Behavior Observations:_____
_____
_____
_____

Fall Migration Notes:_____
_____

Date of Last Hummingbird:_____

Hummingbird Journal

Year: _____

Date of First Hummingbird: _____

Spring Migration Notes: _____
_____

Other Significant Dates: _____
_____

Plants Hummingbirds Preferred: _____
_____
_____

Other Habitat Changes and Notes: _____
_____
_____

Hummingbird Behavior Observations: _____
_____
_____
_____

Fall Migration Notes: _____
_____

Date of Last Hummingbird: _____

Hummingbird Journal

Year: _____

Date of First Hummingbird: _____

Spring Migration Notes: _____
_____

Other Significant Dates: _____
_____

Plants Hummingbirds Preferred: _____
_____
_____

Other Habitat Changes and Notes: _____
_____
_____

Hummingbird Behavior Observations: _____
_____
_____
_____

Fall Migration Notes: _____
_____

Date of Last Hummingbird: _____

Index